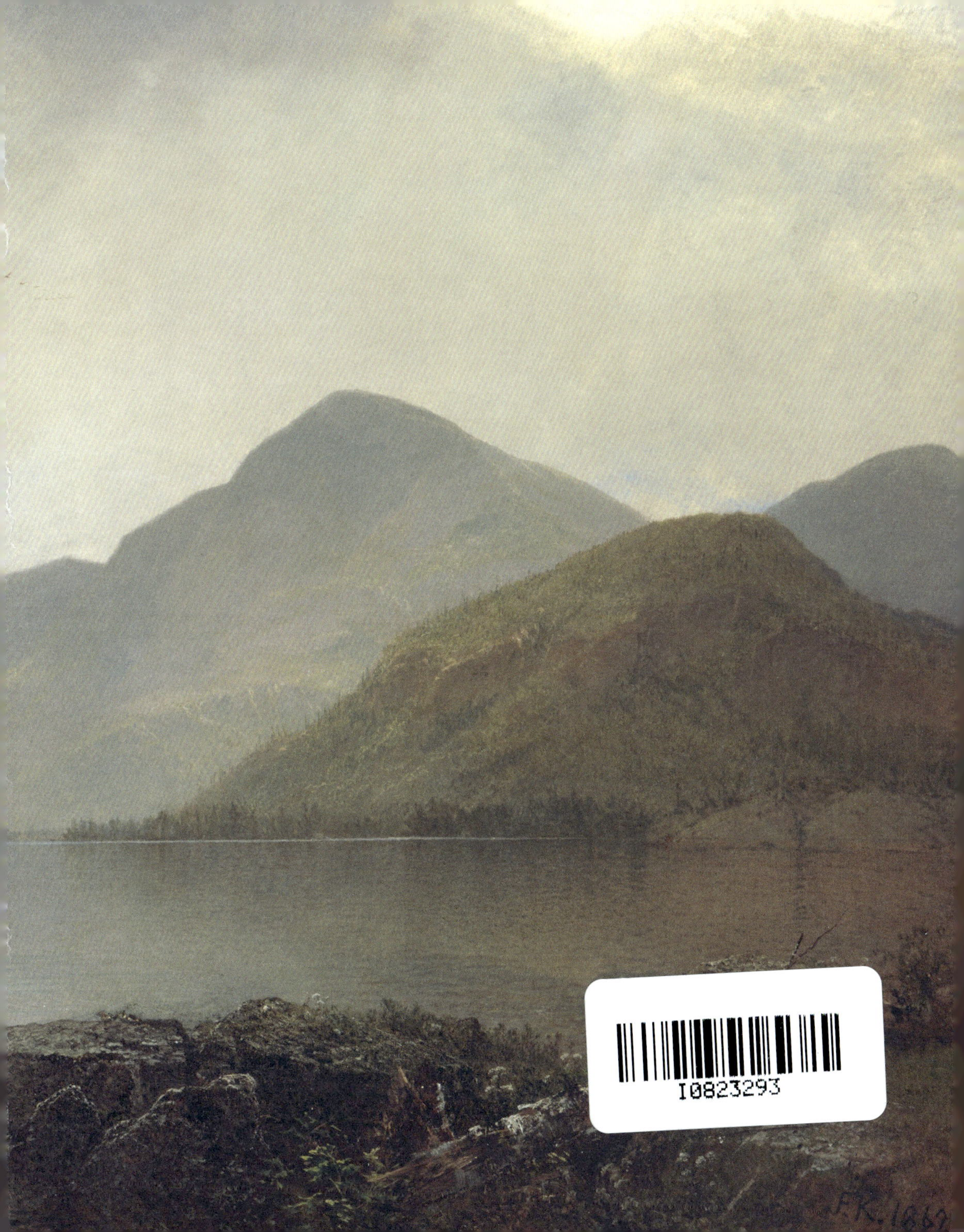

I0823293

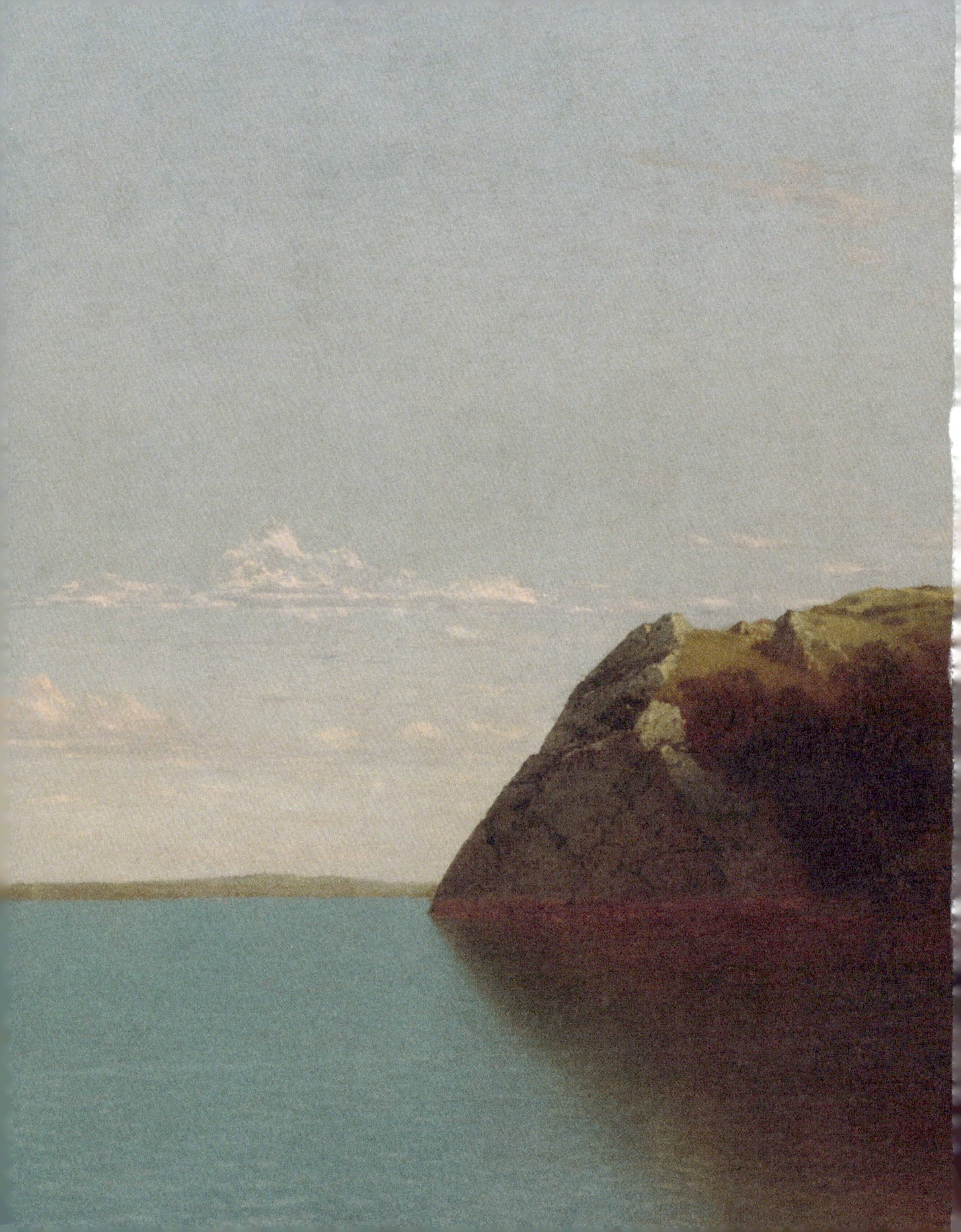

THE INNER LIFE OF THE ARTIST

CONVERSATIONS FROM THE ATELIER

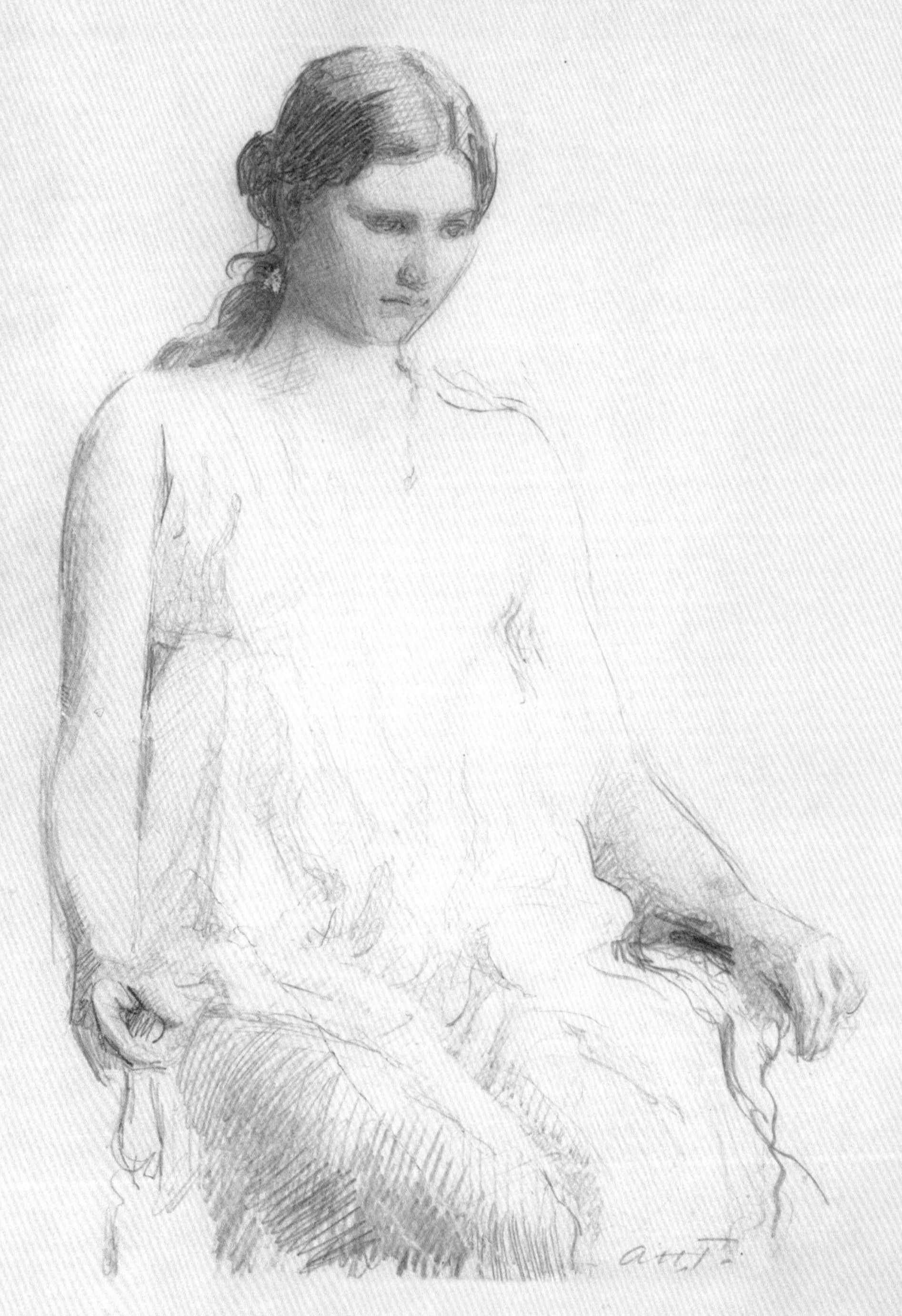

THE INNER LIFE OF THE ARTIST

CONVERSATIONS FROM THE ATELIER

Juliette Aristides

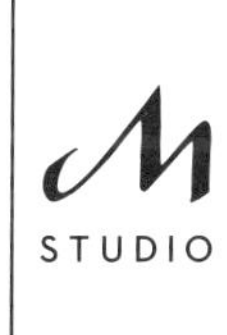

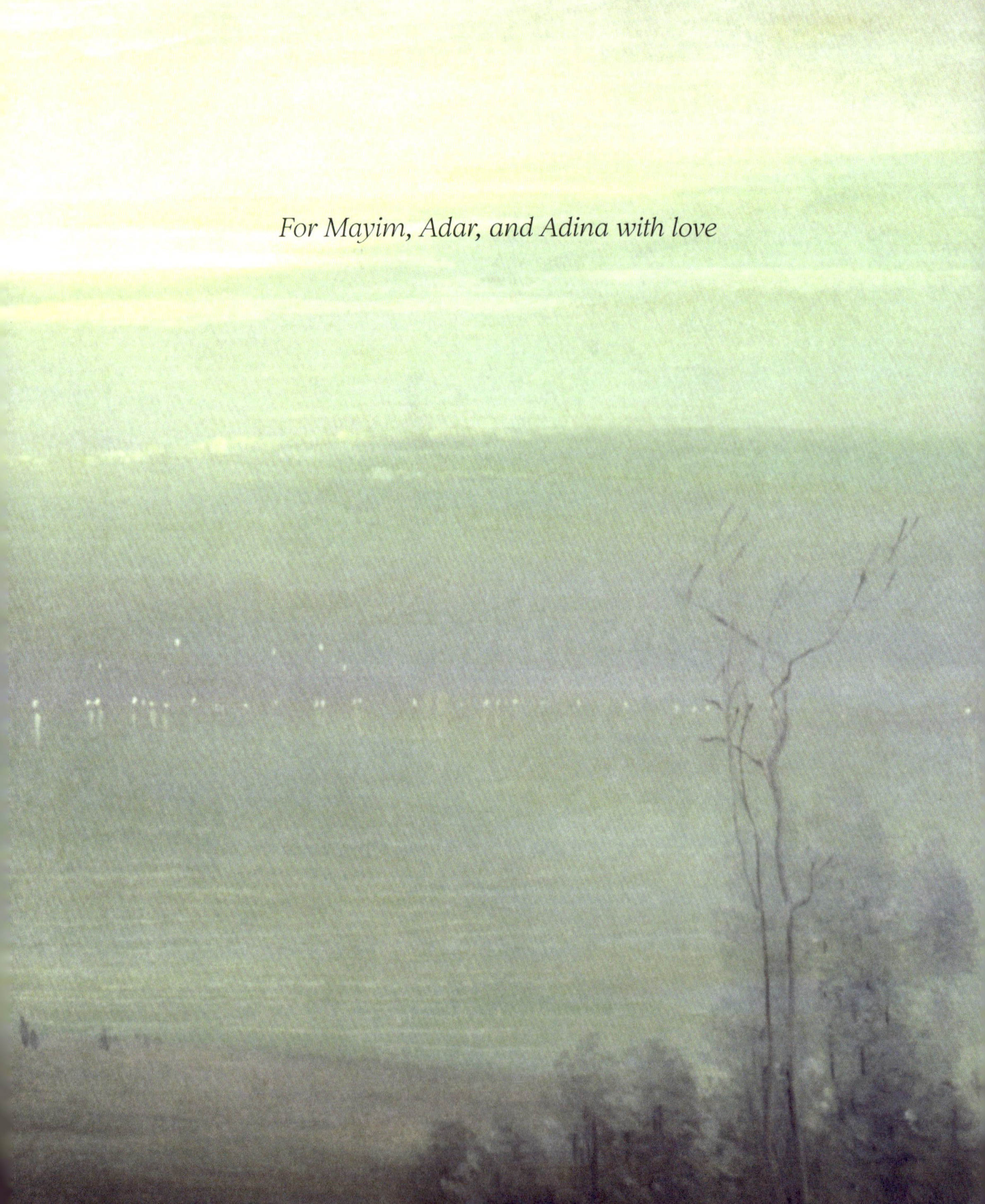

For Mayim, Adar, and Adina with love

TABLE OF CONTENTS

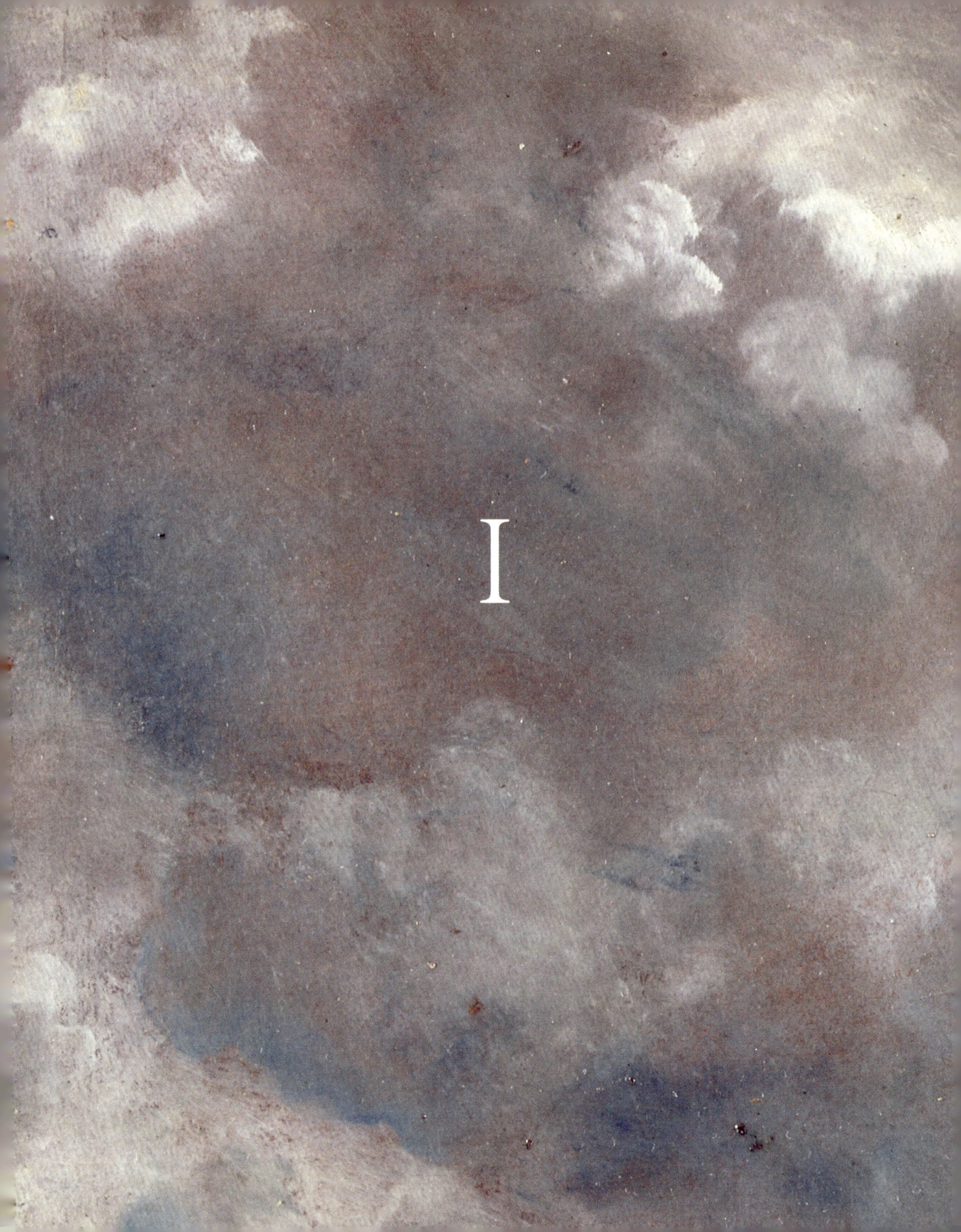

I

THE ARTIST'S PILGRIMAGE

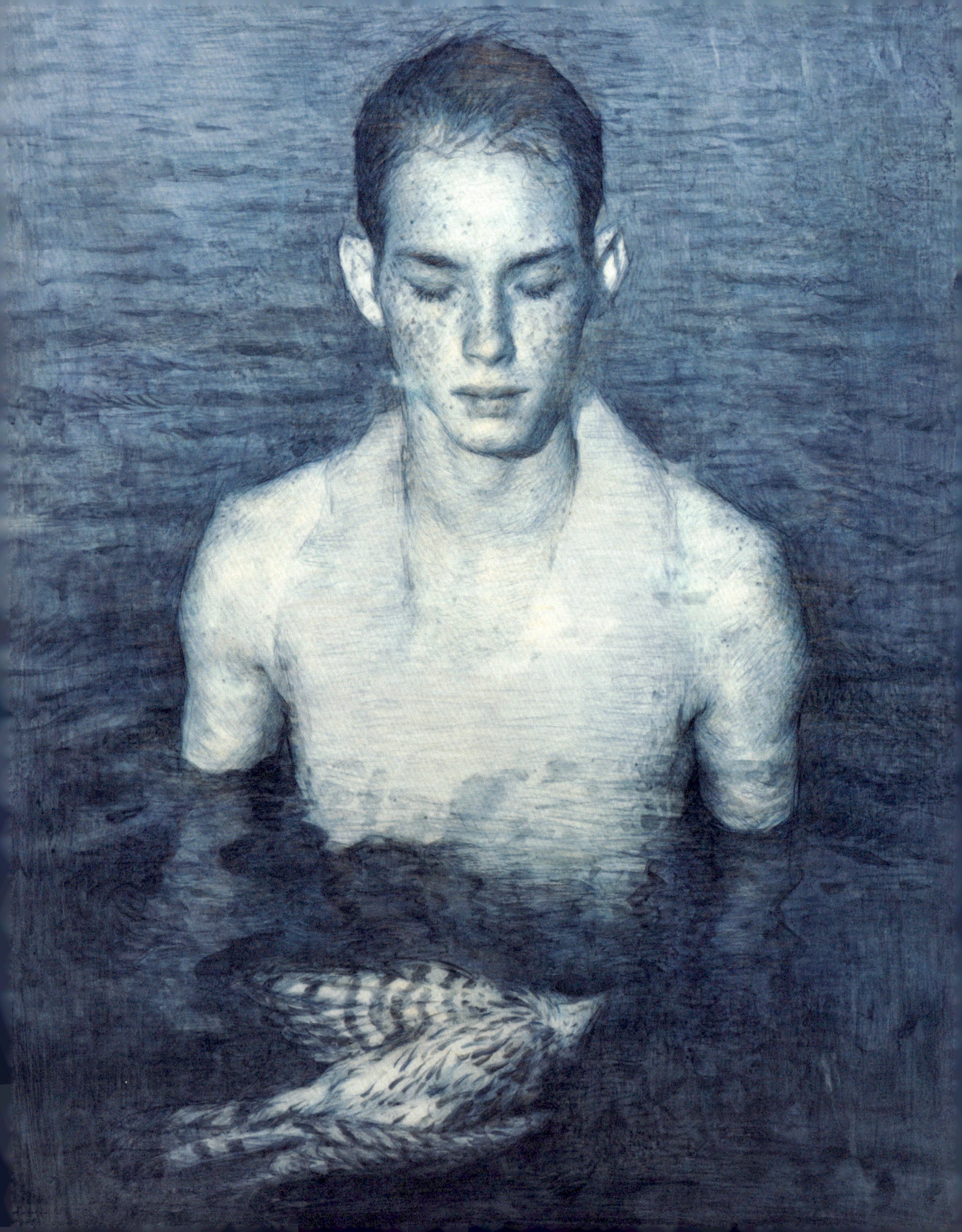

A CATHEDRAL IN MY MIND

We live but a fraction of our life.
Why do we not let on the flood.
Employ your senses.
—HENRY DAVID THOREAU

ARTIFICIAL INTELLIGENCE could write this book for me by the time I drink a cup of coffee, yet it has taken me my whole life to say these words. I could also have someone live my life for me and wake me up when it's over. But I choose to live my own life, think my own thoughts, and make my own mistakes.

I am now a citizen of two worlds: the real physical one and one digitally mediated. You could say I am living in the interdigital age.

There is a strong case to be made for developing the parts of ourselves that lead nowhere in particular. After all, the laws of movement in nature are curved, not linear. The seasons loop in perpetual motion, just like the planets and just like the hours in a day. Yet we strain against this limitation. We want to go forward, not around.

There is no quick way to enlarge a soul. Efficiency and perfection mean nothing to the part of ourselves that longs for a deep connection and a peek behind the veil of the world. How can we know which experiences will contribute to our growth?

Preserving the solitary, literate part of ourselves from a network of continual connectivity is an essential for our creative life.

Imagine this time as a nature preserve of sorts, except it's a preserve for attention—just as endangered as any animal. To paint what we see with our eyes is as John Berger wrote "an act of resistance instigating hope." I include all activities which set our mind to beauty and require the skillful use of our hands. Stone by stone, choice by choice, we build a cathedral in our minds.

OPEN THE DOOR TO EXPERIENCE

It's easy to slide into habit, to shut and bolt the door to opportunities outside our immediate interests. We must open the door wide to experience. It makes a difference what we talk about, read, and watch because we conform to the likeness of what we consume.

There are many ways we can enlarge our lives without leaving our front door. Learning to draw is one of the quickest ways to transform how we see. Drawing creates friction; it slows down the immediacy of sight. Doing things by hand, like writing and drawing, expands our ability to pay attention.

By narrowing human experience to only the useful, we risk destroying the fragile ecosystem that enlarges us. When I bought my first book of essays, I didn't know that it would inspire me to write them or that studying would lead me to teach.

My father was a doctor. Now he merges his desire to heal others with street photography and psychology. This evolution happened naturally as he followed a lifelong curiosity about the world around him. Taking paths that seem to lead nowhere allows us to innovate and meet ourselves in disguise.

When we put pen to paper, fingers to piano keys, eyes to great books, we cultivate the art of being human. Each skill builds a lattice of connection. Below are a few activities that change me for the better.

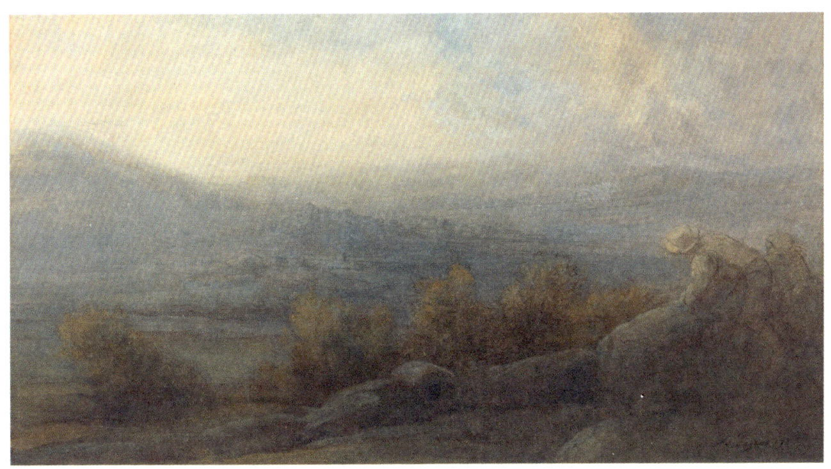

I write to think.
I read to write.
I draw to see.
I daydream to grow.

Achievement, imperfect or otherwise, adds depth to our height and width.

Making, learning, and creating are generative processes. The more we learn, the more we are capable of learning. The desire to create comes from the discipline of working just as the feelings of love follow the actions of love. The hunger to learn and the capacity to do it spin like the rotation of a wheel in quick succession until cause and effect are indistinguishable.

You are the true subject of your art. We only become worthy of our calling by following it. How do you become an artist? Choose to be one and never stop. You don't need anyone's permission but your own.

This is messy—so love the mess, if you can. In the spirit of growth, let's waste a little time and embrace all that makes us human along the way.

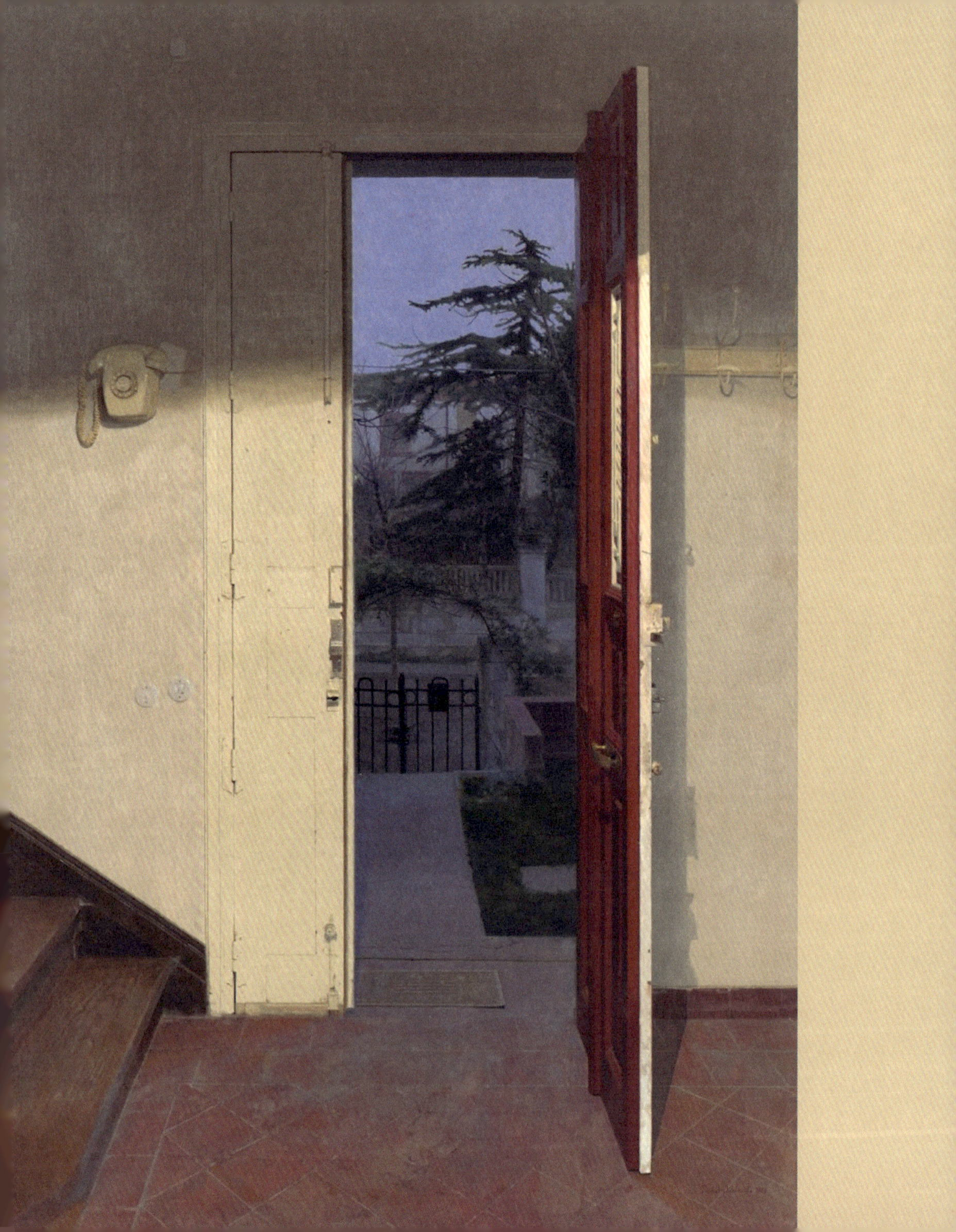

BEGINNINGS

To rediscover astonishment.
What we need to question is bricks, concrete . . .
To question that which seems
to cease forever to astonish us.

—GEORGES PEREC

I GREW UP IN A HOUSE THAT MY PARENTS BUILT in the Pennsylvania woods opening onto farmers' fields. On my walks, I crushed sassafras leaves and mayflowers and trailed through fields of compact soil. I felt alert and beautifully invisible. The part of myself starved in company was fed when I was alone. As Jean-Jacques Rousseau wrote, "These hours of solitude and meditation are the only ones when I am entirely myself . . . when I can truly say, I am what nature designed me." As I got older, paintings, books, and poems gave me the same freedom and led me to the same threshold.

As a kid, I was often bored and excruciatingly shy. All pretense to extroversion started as a dare to myself, much like parachuting out of an airplane would challenge a different sort of person. The cell phone had yet to be invented, and although we had TV, I was almost never allowed to watch it. Rousseau became a good role model. He vowed to step off the ladder of ambition at age forty to spend the rest of his life taking barometric readings of his soul. At seventeen, I thought that was unbelievably cool and decided to do the same.

Somewhere in the boredom, the world of ideas burst upon me with surprise. I started writing and sketching. In the true spirit of Romanticism, I worked alone at night when everyone was asleep. I snuck out of my house and rolled the car out of the driveway, holding my breath to start the engine until I could no longer be heard. I was off to an all-night diner with my pencil and notebook. Knowing my parents would kill me added an extra thrill of being unfairly persecuted.

With my pencil in hand, I approached the sensation of thought circuitously lest I chase it away. These fledgling thoughts flickered and went dark, but occasionally the fuse would catch and I experienced the ecstasy of original ideas. In truth, this was my first exposure to what it feels like to make art.

Curiosity is an artistic prime mover. The best questions are ones that can't be answered by an internet search but set our hearts on a pilgrimage. And as with any pilgrim's journey, it isn't only the arrival that's important but also the setting forth. We leave the familiar, wandering and struggling to encounter something holy and profound. We make sense of it, if at all, later.

You embark on the path of the artist by yourself and yet not alone. There are fellow sojourners from every age who hear a call and follow it. Who are these other travelers? Of old, their paintings hang on the walls of museums or their books rest by our bedsides. Or today, they may be in kitchens tinkering with sauces. We may catch a glimpse of their gardens on a walk or see them staring idly out windows. These artists, in every medium, preserve the human within us and what is most likely to be lost in the world at large.

The most impressive artists I know look completely ordinary. You could pass them in the street and not notice. All their energy is

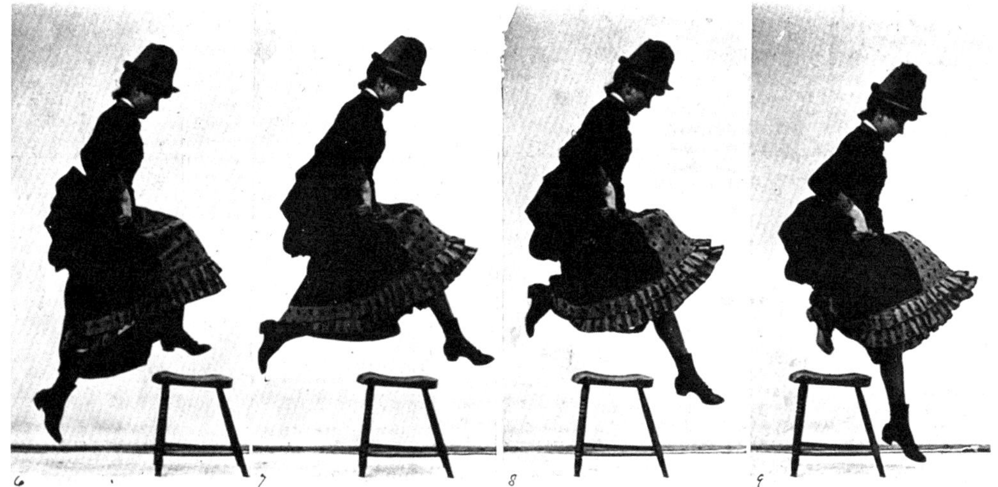

directed inward. Artists often need little outside of their own heads to begin, so you have everything you require right now to join them.

How do you and I create an artistic path for ourselves? How do we illuminate the things in our hearts that we feel but don't see? Sonar reveals the shape and placement of things hidden in the darkness by sending out pulses of sound to measure the depth and length from the returning vibrations. Likewise, we must notice our own points of resonance.

In the process of looking, reading, listening, conversing, a picture emerges of who we are and what we care about. We form our own opinions about the world and our own original thoughts take shape.

So as you begin your training in art, remember you were called long before your formal studies began. Before you had anyone's approval, you sensed it in a wordless place inside you. You sent sound waves into the world and came to know the shape of things all on your own. Follow your curiosity. Your questions and longing will illuminate the invisible and add something new and beautiful to the world. In a word, *Art*.

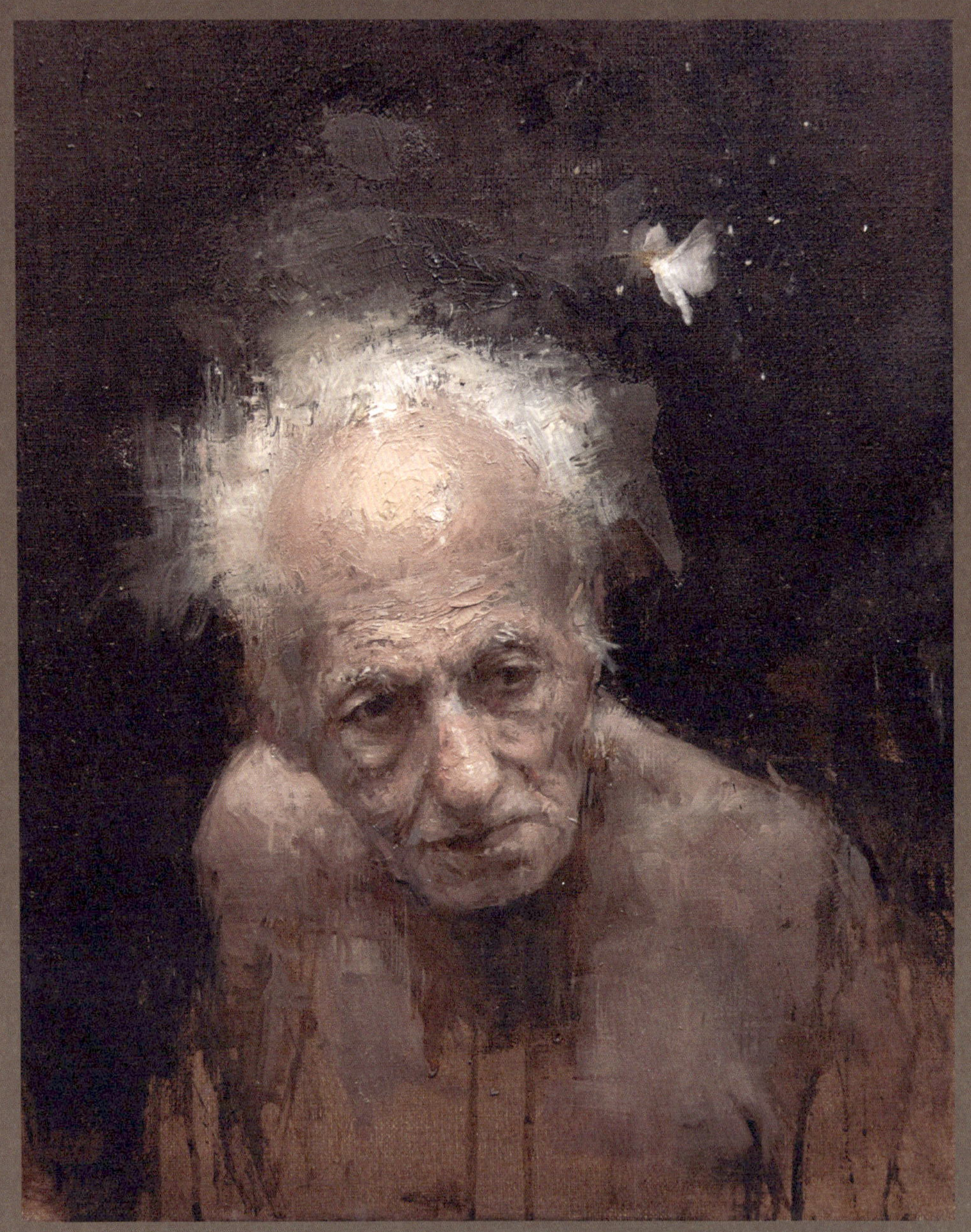

A man should learn to detect
and watch
that gleam that flashes
across his mind from within.

—RALPH WALDO EMERSON

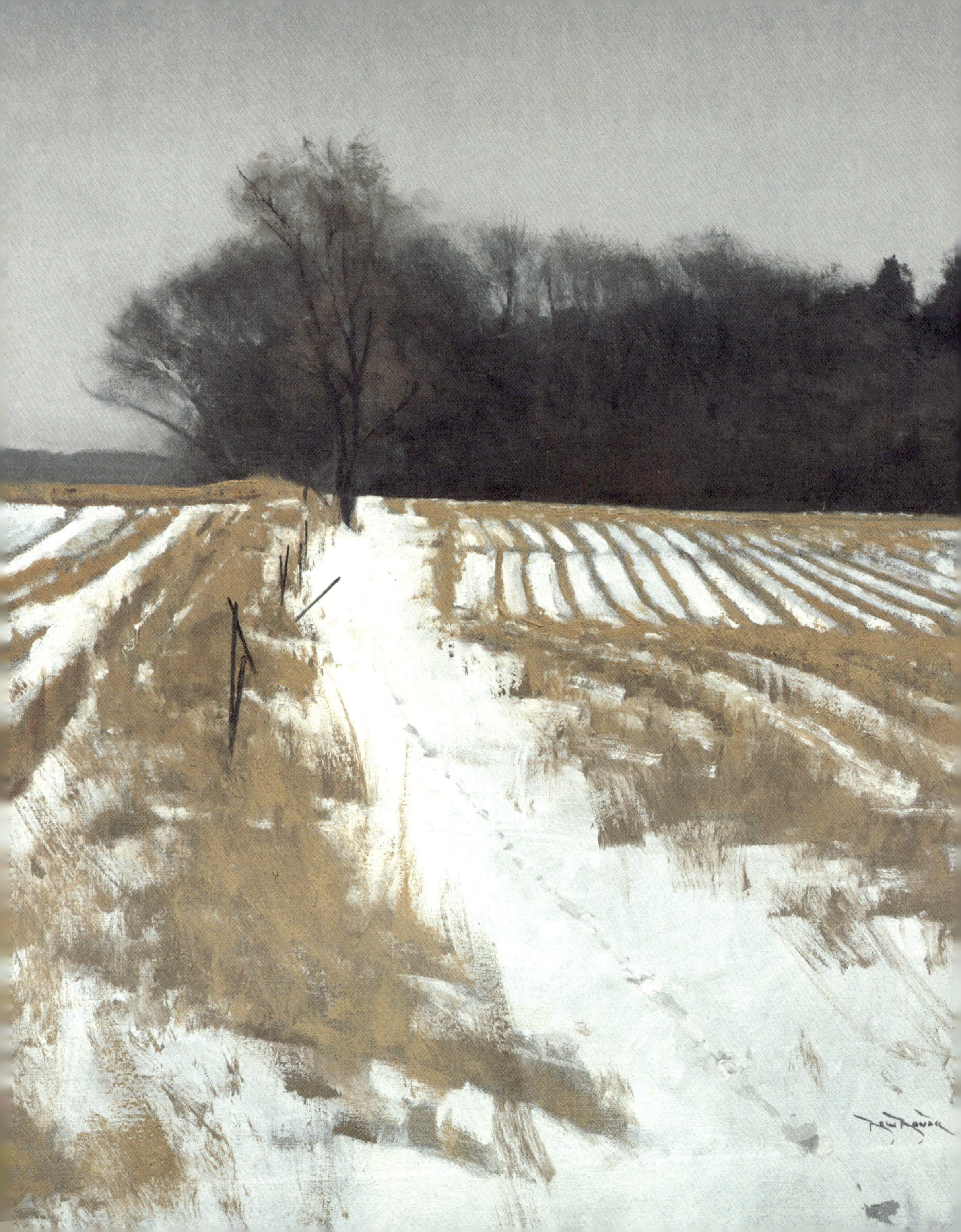

WAYSIDE SACRAMENT

Never lose an opportunity
of seeing anything that is beautiful;
for beauty is God's handwriting—
a wayside sacrament.
—RALPH WALDO EMERSON

AFTER A PARTICULARLY TOUGH START to the school year, I took a quick winter holiday from Seattle to a rural mountain town. That night, right before bed, I realized I had left something I needed in my car and went to get it. The complete darkness outside came as a surprise. It was perfectly silent: everything covered with a mountain of snow and the snow was still falling.

I turned on my flashlight and shone a searchlight into the sky. In the beam of light, the snowflakes went the wrong direction: they drifted up instead of down.

I held my breath so as not to move a muscle—I was on holy ground.

Most of my experiences of beauty are not in a museum, cathedral, or concert hall; they are not high art or a peak experience or a view from the mountaintop. They are very small points of heightened awareness. It is the milk in my coffee forming a galaxy as it spins, the streetlight casting shadows against the wall from the pottery in my kitchen window or the fluttering of leaves on a branch.

There are times when it is easy to see beauty, for example when the rising sun makes the sky a canvas of rose and gold. Likewise, it's hard to miss the giant Tiepolo at the top of the stairs of the Metropolitan Museum of Art because we walk right toward it and it's enormous.

The beauty of nature is a free gift. We don't need any particular sensitivity; we just raise our hand to catch it. Yet can we find beauty in subtler circumstances?

If we see the beauty of a mountain, can we also find it in a puddle. If a baby's angelic face makes my chest swell, do I also have the capacity to be moved by a face skewed by age? Herein lies the challenge.

What small, beautiful, invisible thing did you notice today that made you feel alive and no one else noticed? When did you find the past disappearing and the worries for tomorrow enveloped in the act of living? Careful observation pulls us into the deep well of artistic vision. These small sources of aesthetic pleasure create a sensibility of wonder that many artists point to as the origin of their art.

Yet if beauty links us more deeply to our own lives, as a wellspring of art and a conduit to the divine, why don't we spend our entire life in that state of bliss? In truth, often we are not sure what to look for.

Thomas Couture, the influential nineteenth-century artist, wanted to initiate his eager students into the secrets of the world's greatest art. They were prepared to be awed. Yet he cautioned them to lower expectations. If he pulls back the curtain to show the secret of beauty in art and nature, they may see nothing. Beauty is so simple it can easily be overlooked. If you look superficially, you will only see the common, yet look deeper to find the sublime.

Sometimes we don't see beauty because life gets in the way. When my daughter put diesel fuel in our unleaded car, there was no beauty that day, only aggravation and expense. Real life is hard, and

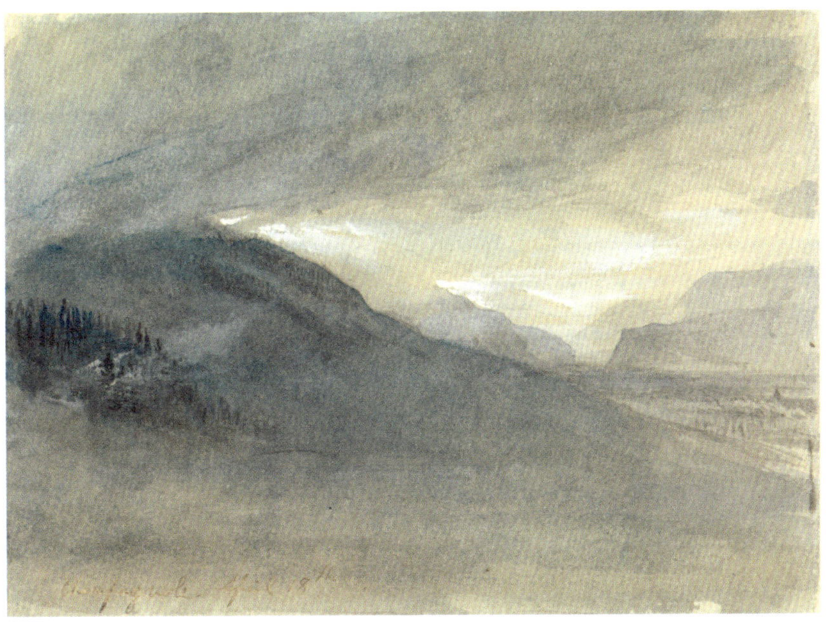

the external world impinges on our happiness in countless ways small and large. Maybe you're the shortest person in the back of a crowd looking at the *Mona Lisa*, or you have to use the bathroom and there is no exit off the freeway, or your school was designed by a brutalist architect on a budget. And these are only mere inconveniences. If beauty weren't so hard to see, hidden by disappointment, distraction, the ordinary, and the brutal, we would all be artists and poets. Even when life is fine, we can still spend our days bracing for impact. Our eyes can grow dark because our hearts are heavy for countless reasons.

Kenneth Clark suggests that just as individuals who see no future will collapse inward, the same is true for civilizations. Civilizations appear strong but are actually quite fragile, and there are many things that can destroy them. Yet art knows what to do with sadness and fear and darkness. Art creates a point of transformation from suffering into objects of meaning and connection. Beauty calls us out of ourselves and into life.

Learning how to see beauty is an act of will. We don't have to start with large gestures; we can find moments of beauty by simply looking for them. Shut your computer, hang up the phone, turn off the music, and grow quiet. Something is demanded of us. Let's adjust to a quieter register and see what is alive inside us. At first you may strain against boredom, but don't evade it. Gradually a taste for the good, healthy soul-affirming will rise up, but you must wait for it—clear your schedule.

We can learn something from "saints of the everyday": Henry David Thoreau made a career of observing things that everyone else walked by. One day he pulled up some grasses and noticed the roots were covered with a kind of crystalline dew. He examined them, feeling them and tasting them (*tasting them?!*). He noticed that grass is beautifully engineered and that in the dirt, out of sight, the most delicate and magical processes are going on. The half is not shown; we must rise to meet it.

> *The moment one gives close attention to anything,*
> *even a blade of grass,*
> *it becomes a mysterious, awesome,*
> *indescribably magnificent world in itself.*
>
> —HENRY MILLER

Now you might be tempted to think that these quotes show an impressive humility, but I suspect they are meant to challenge a material age. "You may be pleased that you see the beauty in a painting, fair enough, yet I can see eternity in a piece of turf."

When you have got quite alone,
sit down and be lonely . . .
fold your hands in your lap, and be still.
Do not try to think of anything . . .
by and by, it may be, you will begin
to know something of nature.
Nature will soon speak to you,
or not until some veil be broken in you.

—GEORGE MACDONALD

If you are quiet enough to see light hitting a wall in long diagonals and if the changing color of fall grasses makes you stop and stare, then you are blessed to see the face of God in his benediction of the ordinary. You *are* already an artist—the rest is just technique.

So, before we part ways, let's stand again with Thomas Couture as he pulls back a curtain to reveal to you the beauty of art and nature. And perhaps this time we find that behind the curtain is your life laid out before you. Do you think it's beautiful? If you look at anything quickly, it's ordinary, but if you slow down and look deeply, you'll see the sublime.

The half isn't shown.

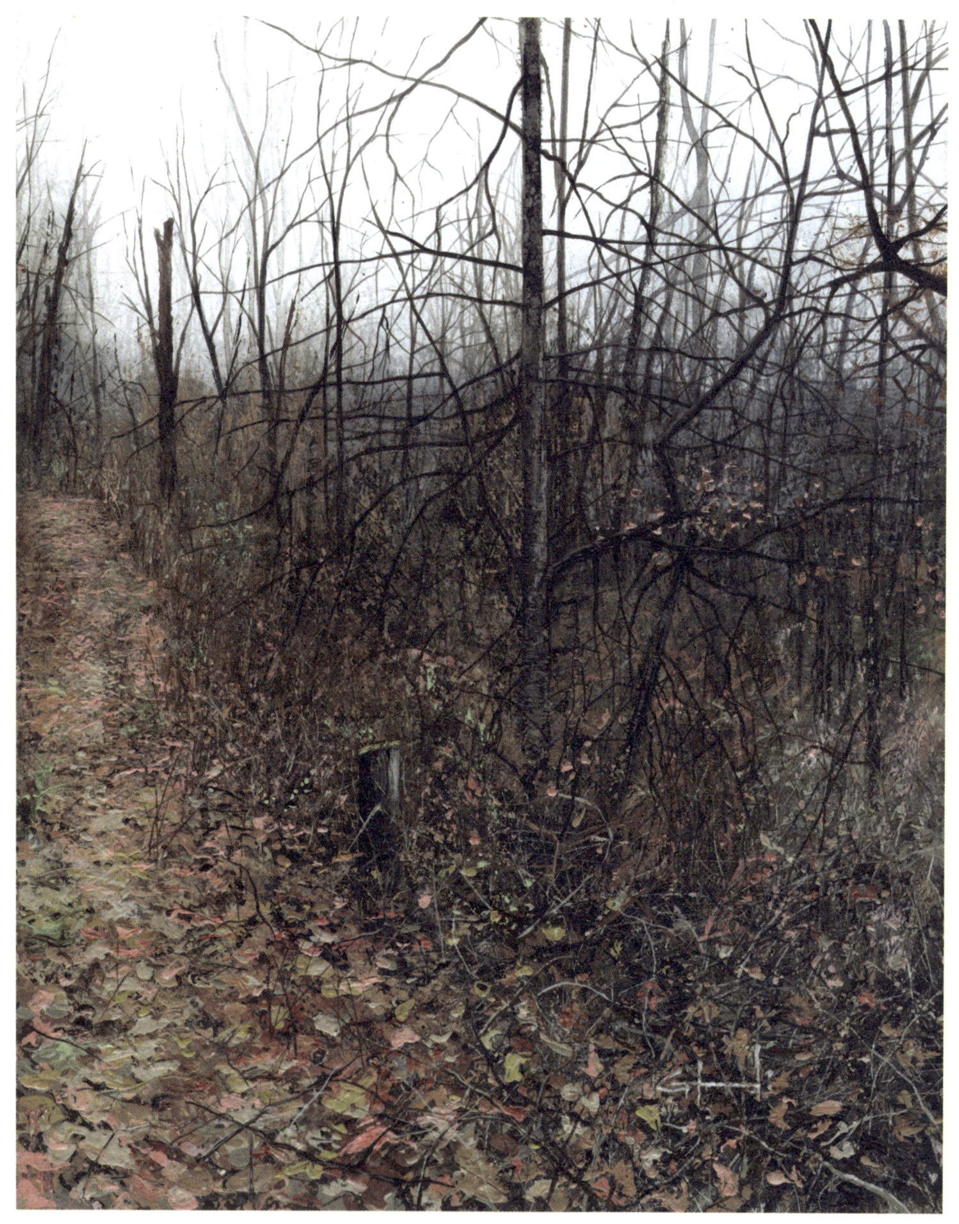

AN EXERCISE OF ATTENTION

So what is noticing?
A pinpoint of awareness,
The detail that stands out amid all the details.
It's catching your sleeve on the thorn
of the thing you notice
And paying attention as you free yourself.
—VERLYN KLINKENBORG

CLOSE FRIEND AND COLLEAGUE artist Mark Kang-O'Higgins is a landscape painter and skilled animal tracker. Our lunchtime walks from the art studio to get coffee were often punctuated by him asking me such questions as: "Did a squirrel or a rat make that tiny, muddy footprint and with which paw?" He had to frequently wait for me to collect interesting leaves and sticks—a mutual dawdling.

I asked him for a practice he uses to teach budding naturalists how to observe more carefully.

THE SIT SPOT

A sit spot is a quiet place to observe the natural world. Go to a natural place—the woods, a meadow, someplace familiar or somewhere new.

If it's a wild place, enter and leave from different directions so you leave no trail.

Look, listen, do nothing, let your eyes grow soft. Be there for about 15 minutes, or more if you feel like it. Let your mind be quiet. Notice birdlife. You may hear many birdcalls and think of them as territorial songs, but they are, at first, often alarms. The sentinels are watching your noisy entrance. In nature humans are the anomaly.

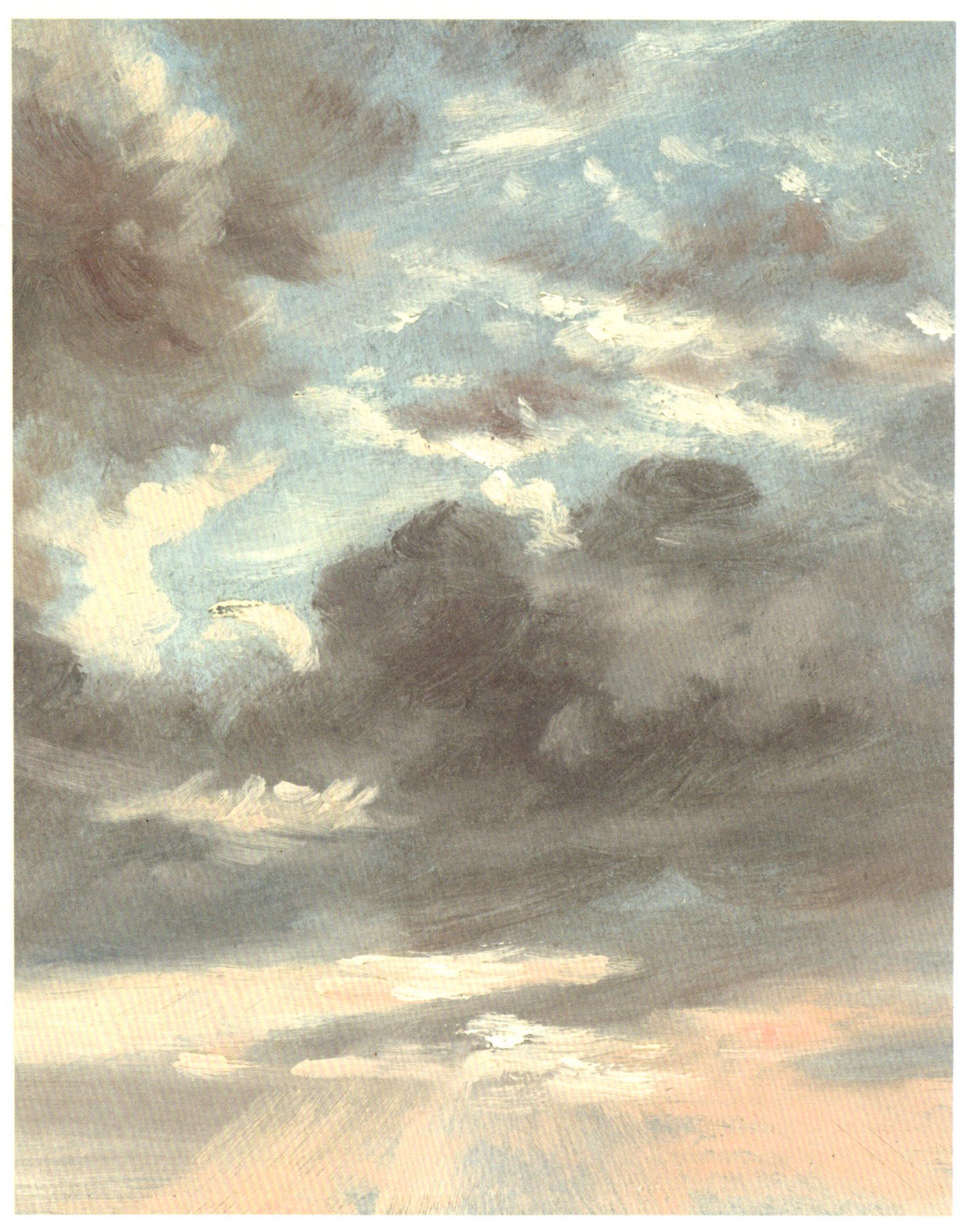

IF YOU SIT QUIETLY FOR A SPELL, they will go back to their normal routine.

ACCLIMATIZE YOURSELF: you are still a guest, but part of their world.

NOW YOU CAN HEAR the disturbances of the forests and the animals as they go about their lives.

THE VERY ACT OF SLOWING DOWN and separating yourself from the practical, the daily, will heighten your perceptions. This is also a big part of the creative endeavor. You are awake, listening. Your mind is open, curious; you are growing and learning all at the same time. Your brain is becoming refreshed and rested. In our oversaturated, noisy, mediated age, you have adjusted your tastes to be simpler, quieter.

YOU BEGIN TO NOTICE.

*I tried this exercise and wrote what I noticed in a notebook. It helped me focus and remember. I was so still that a hummingbird hovered right in front of my nose.

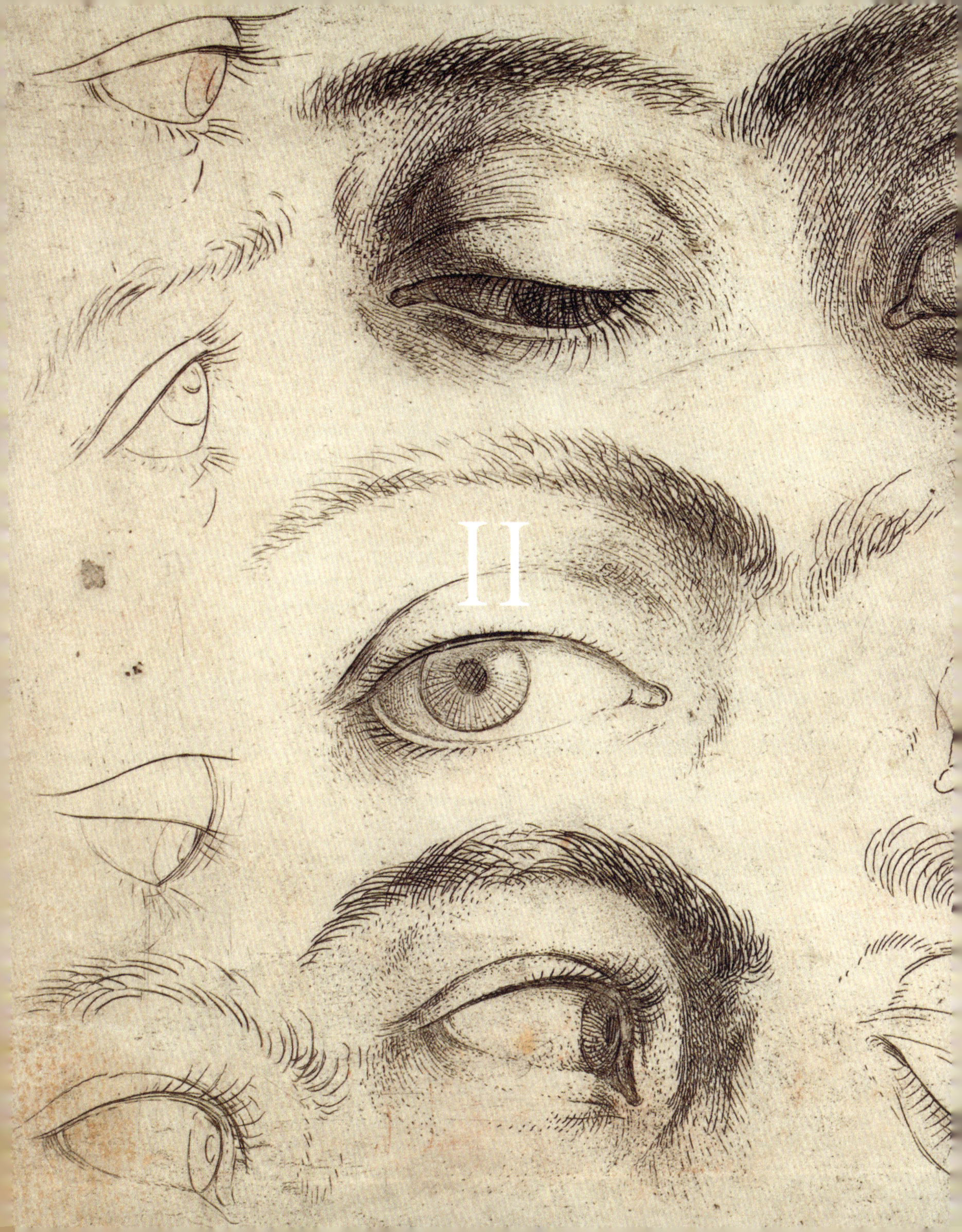

II

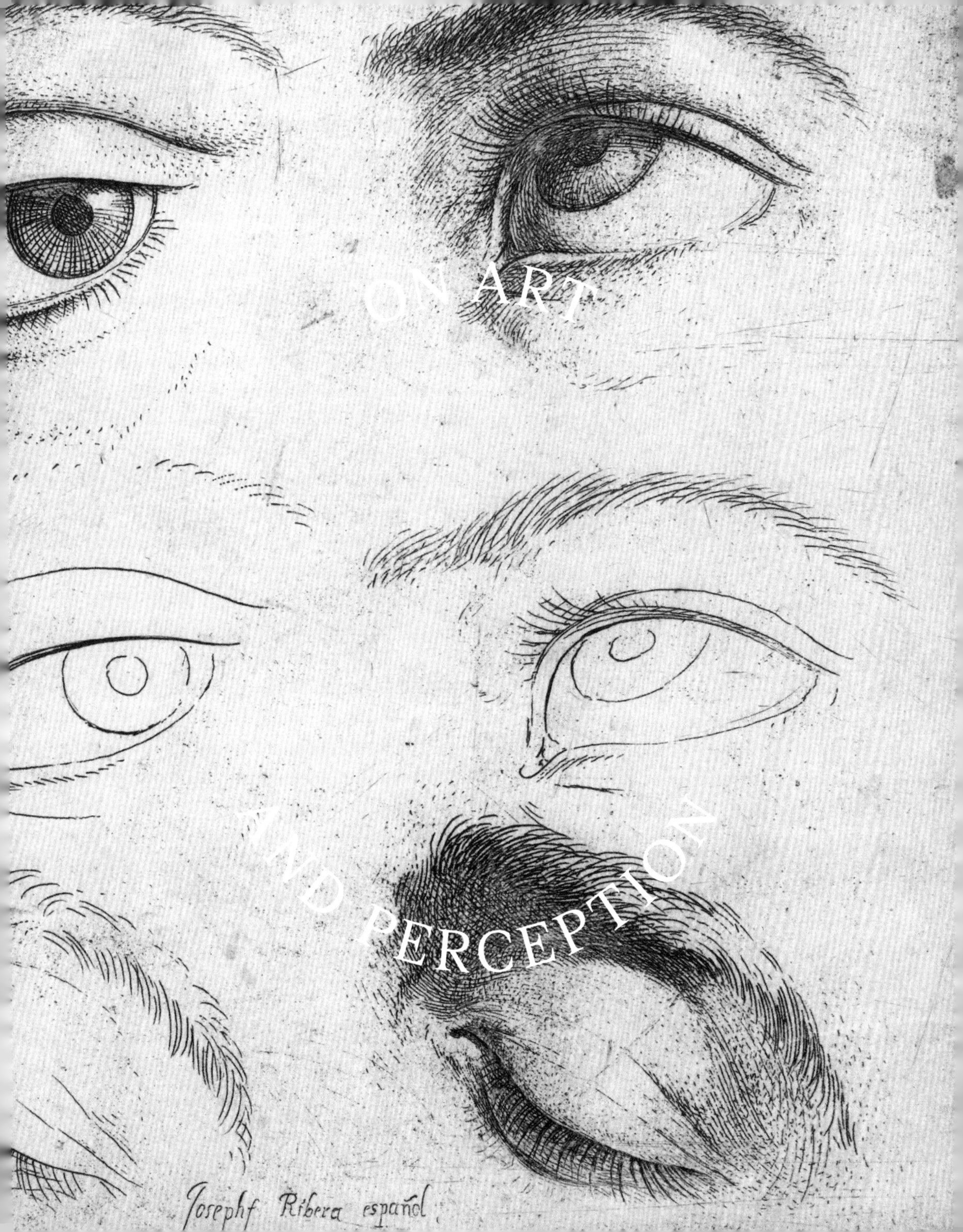
ON ART
AND PERCEPTION
Josephf Ribera español

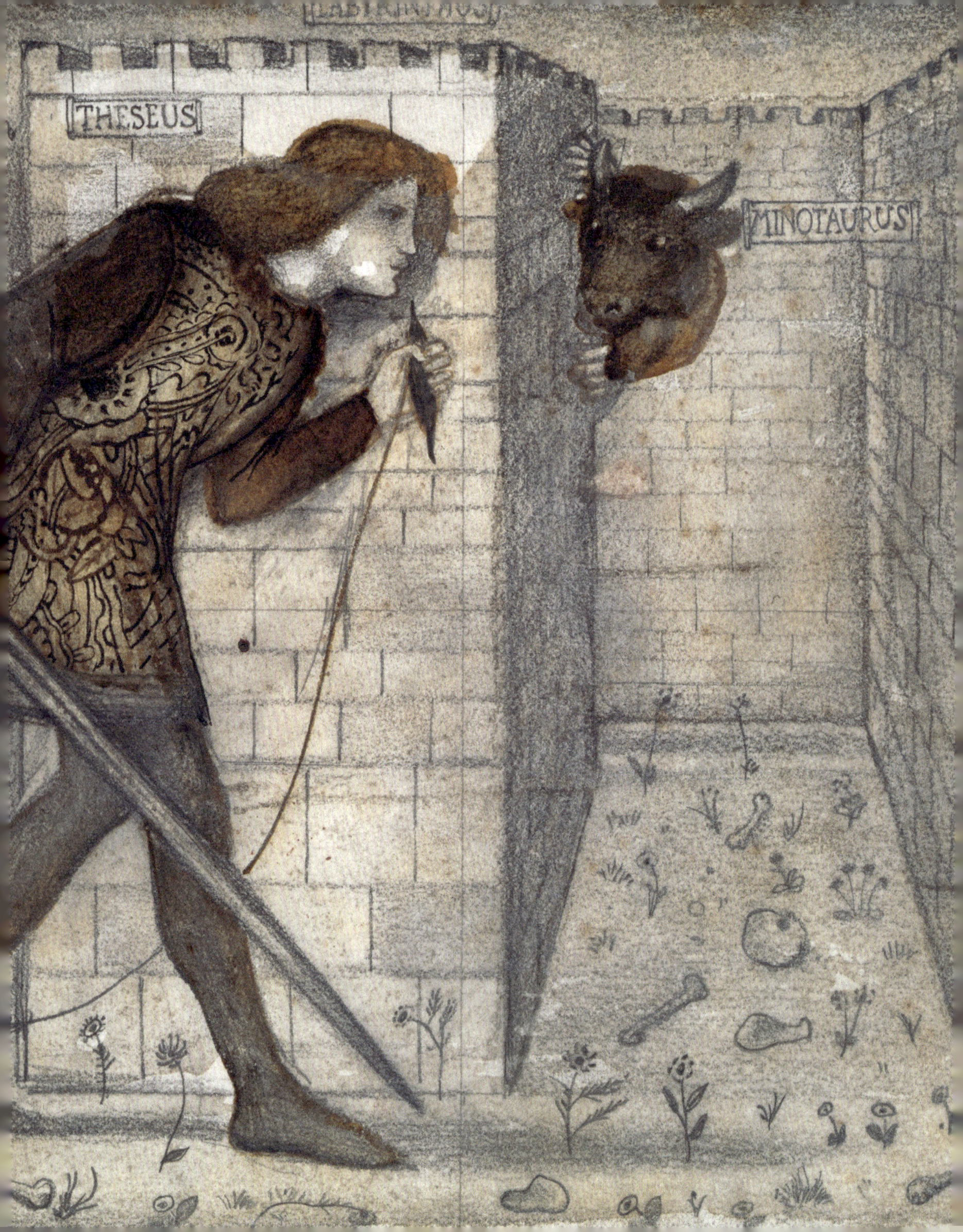
THESEUS
MINOTAURUS

LABYRINTH

Our horizons need not be vast
for battles to be important,
and the most curious events and revolutions
take place beneath the firmament of the skull,
in the close and mysterious
laboratory of the brain.

—CHARLES BAUDELAIRE

OPPOSITE MY OLD ART STUDIO there's a flagstone copy of the labyrinth at Chartres Cathedral that offers a pilgrimage in miniature. I spent some time studying it. It appears to be a quick walk to the center of the labyrinth, straight as the crow flies. It's unicursal—a single winding path—so unlike a maze, you can't get lost. However, it's deceptively simple.

I aim directly toward the center of the labyrinth and am quickly routed the other direction. There are switchbacks and tight curves leading to straight stretches that throw off my orientation. One minute I'm heading to my goal, and the next I am looping back to the start. It's disorienting, monotonous, and straightforward progress is impossible. Perhaps I mistakenly walked in the wrong lane? It's tempting to just leave—why not? Eventually, I decide to just enjoy the walk. Then, I reach the center. It came to meet me.

Perhaps all the Dragons in our lives are princesses
who are only waiting
to see us once beautiful and brave.
—RAINER MARIA RILKE

At the start of a new Atelier year, I recommend that students walk the labyrinth. It offers a taste of the challenges of artistic training and also the key to achieving it. The difficulty in gaining artistic mastery isn't a glitch in the process; it *is* the process in its entirety. It requires transformation and not only of the hand and eye. You are physically and mentally different by the end of it.

Like ancient myths, we must expect to meet minotaurs along the way. They appear in many forms: as a force of resistance which rises in opposition to us; as procrastination, self-doubt, a shortage of time and money, jealousy or careless words of other people; or simply, as a subtle negation.

In the dark of the labyrinth, you can feel lost while being on the right path. There are times when you can't trust your eyes and must follow a thread that no one knows is there, but you. On paper, the journey is always easy. Yet, it's not a maze and you won't get lost.

Troubles will come; that is the nature of travel, from the word *travail* for "agonizing effort." If becoming an artist looked easy when I started, it was because I was so young. I had a straight line of sight only because I never looked over the edge to see the labyrinth between myself and the goal. However, in the end, it's just one long walk.

Much in this process won't be under your control. Yet what *can* you control? You can show up; you can hold the thread no matter where it leads. Trust the ancient process that shapes you and the voice that calls you to follow the thread.

LABYRINTH MEDITATION

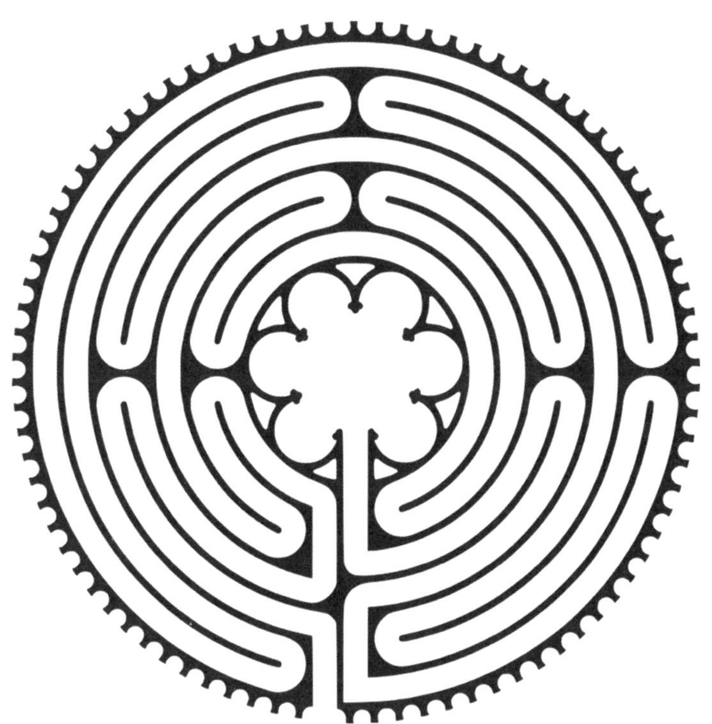

TRY THE LABYRINTH. Use the back of a pen to follow along. Notice the concentration, how long it takes, how it disorients us. How do you deal with that frustration? Now imagine walking it full-scale. Now imagine walking it underground in the dark while following a string and fighting monsters. That is the artist's journey.

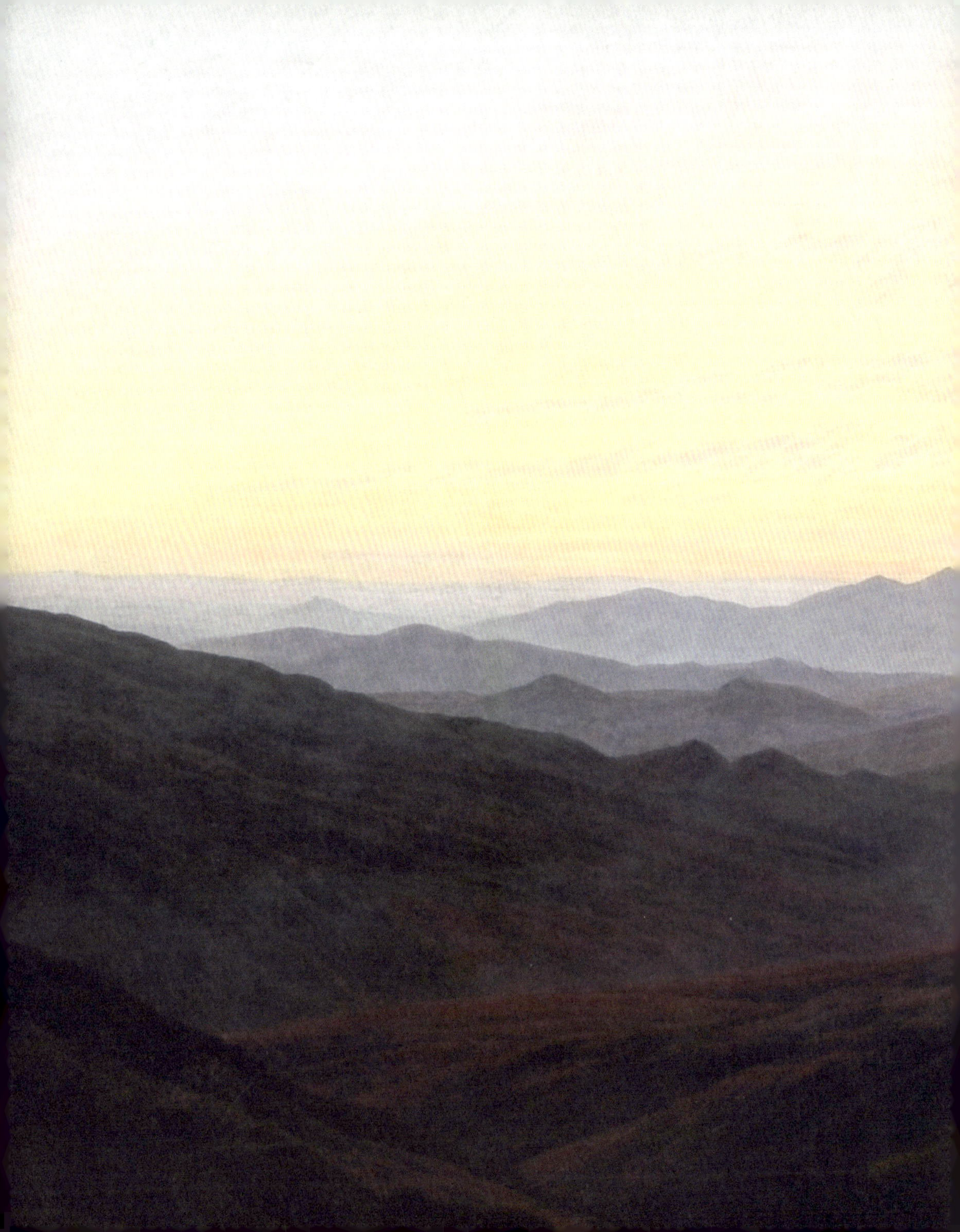

THE SILVER THREAD

ONCE UPON A TIME, there was a young princess who lived in a castle on a mountain. She was loved by all who knew her and protected as long as she stayed within the castle walls. Yet no one told her about the great danger lurking just outside. A kingdom of evil goblins lived in the black, tangled tunnels under the mountain intent on harming those from the sunlit world above. At night these evil creatures roamed freely, catching the innocent whom they dragged into the darkness.

One rainy day the bored princess explored the farthest parts of the castle. Climbing to the top of an abandoned tower, she opened a splintered door to see a great-great-grandmother spinning thread in an empty room. This elder turned and warned her not to go outside. Yet if she was ever in danger to follow the thread, as thin as a spider's web, invisible to all but her to guide her safely home.

One night, a strange creature woke the sleeping princess and scared her out onto the mountainside where she was quickly lost. Remembering the great-great-grandmother's words, she felt for the thread to lead her home. However, instead of turning toward the safety of the castle, the thread led her into a crack in the earth down into the land of the goblins.

Just imagine the doubt and confusion she felt when that thread disappeared into the black earth!

Even worse, as she followed the thread, it went into a wall of rock. Certainly her great-great-grandmother couldn't have meant for her to dig? Yet the princess followed the thread, in faith and not by sight, deeper into the rocks. Eventually, a cave opened revealing a young miner held prisoner. The princess liberated the miner and returned to the sunlit world. In heading toward certain danger, she had avoided it and rose to meet her calling.

THIS STORY IS RETOLD FROM THE 19TH-CENTURY WRITER GEORGE MADONALD, *THE PRINCESS AND CURDIE*, PERHAPS A NOD TO THE ANCIENT MYTH OF THESEUS AND THE MINOTAUR IN THE LABYRINTH.

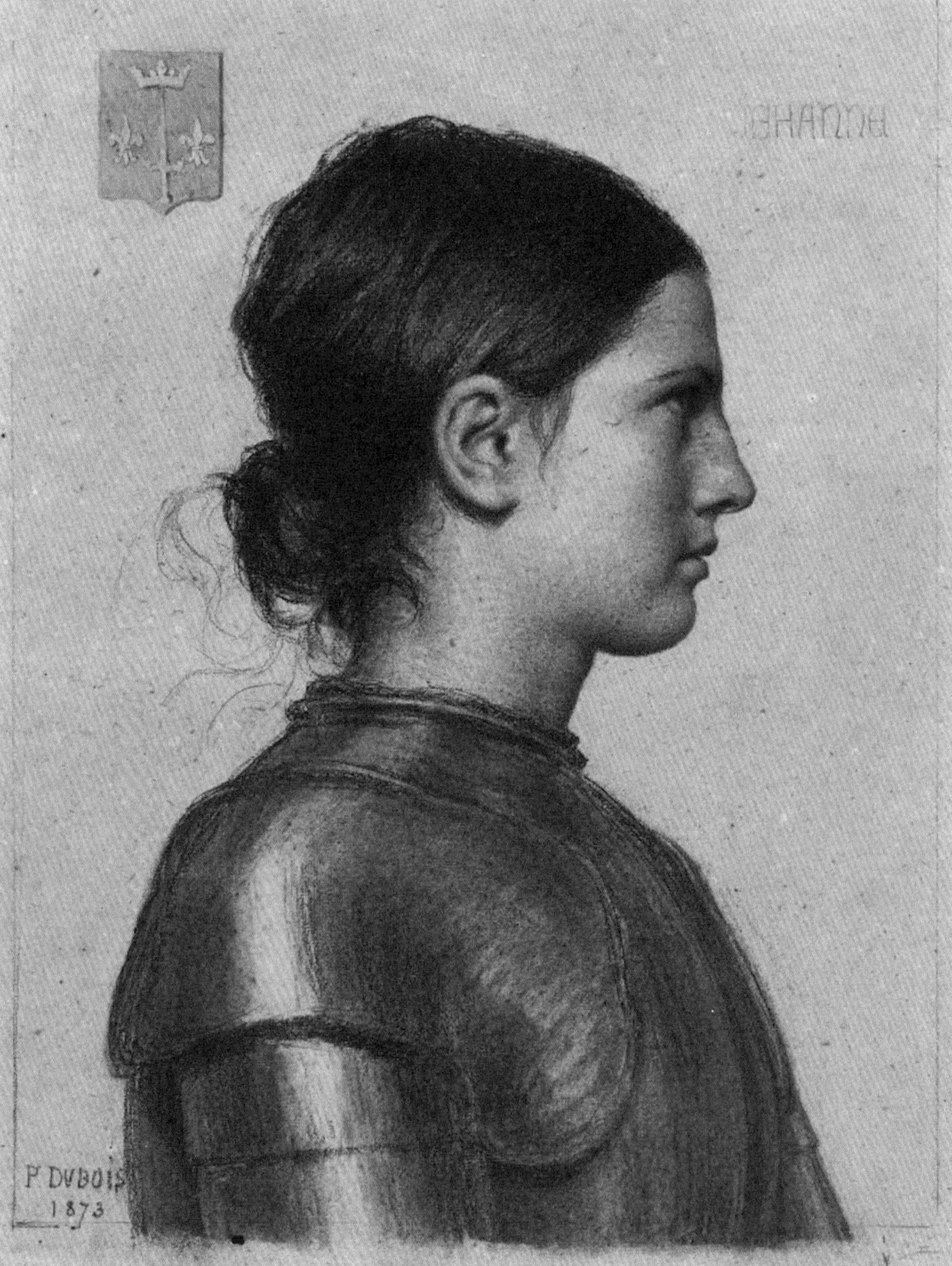
P. DUBOIS
1873

ON INFLUENCE

There are no new recipes. It's like painting.
You are copying a Michelangelo,
but you put a little of yourself in it, too.

—CHEF ANGELO GARRO

WHO WOULDN'T APPRECIATE being applauded as a lone genius whose originality of thought electrifies a culture, the artist with no teachers, yet many followers? The Romantic revolution of the eighteenth century created what is still accepted as our ideal of the artist: the temperamental, solo creator who shuns convention, lit from within only by the force of their own genius. This artistic persona is deeply appealing—all the more so if she's riding a motorcycle. However, in reality this persona is essentially a fiction. We are all shaped by the things that touch our lives. This essay is in praise of something less sensational, less self-referential: the importance of imitation. Simply said, we learn best by copying—so copy. But choose your mentors wisely.

Our culture is a contradiction: We crave novelty while passively watching it on our phones, seemingly unaware of that which quietly shapes us for better or for worse. By denying the power of influence we are most vulnerable to its manipulations. We naturally conform to the likeness of what surrounds us. Marshall McLuhan remarked, "Environments are invisible. Their ground rules are pervasive, their structure and overall patterns elude easy perception."

When everyone wants to be unique, it is those that aim for the ancient virtues of diligence, patience, wisdom, and hope that now seem different. McLuhan suggests that it's the artist as an outsider that has an advantage of seeing what others are habituated to.

For simplicity, we often frame the world by opposites: science or art, creation or destruction, innovation or stagnation. But life doesn't exist in states of perfect polarities. Extremes toggle in life and nature like a contronym—we see opposites reconcile when a doctor is skilled in the "art" of medicine or a disease becomes the cure through a vaccine. We may believe that one is either a teacher or student, but the best teachers often have an insatiable curiosity. Copying and creating are a generative engine.

Learning through immersive exposure is one of the best ways to gain information because you are engaging your senses and practicing. If you want to learn to cook, watch your parents or grandparents in the kitchen, or step it up and work under a chef. A favorite dish of mine growing up was potato latkes. We never needed a recipe because the taste is remembered from childhood and woven into cultural memory. There is a fixed form, true to type, yet it is malleable, subject to endless innovation. The change and adaptability are a sign of its life and relevance. My latkes are sometimes made with zucchini and chives, sometimes with sweet potatoes and sour cream or whatever I try next. It is an interpretation—a master copy with the original lost to time and memory.

The concept of imitation leading to innovation can be easily understood through the lens of language. We are born mimicking speech and the babbling of infancy slides gradually into actual words with intentional meaning. By adulthood, we command tens of thousands of words which are spun into the magic of new sentences. Creativity explodes in every corner of the world through singing, writing, poetry, and books. Copying and creating are spontaneously generative. After all, when we learn to speak and read, we aren't being derivative; we are conversant and literate.

The mythology of the self-taught genius thrives on the illusion that mastery is achievable without effort, that learning should be easy and mistakes are failures. Thomas Edison said, when making the light bulb, "I have not failed. I've just found 10,000 ways that won't work." Generations of potential artists and poets are robbed of an artistic inheritance because they are not given teachers. It's just as silly to imagine we would be born knowing how to read. Accomplishment is always on the far side of hard work—even in the arts.

Artists are not just technicians: All of life goes into making us who we are and likewise all of us funnels back into the work. Let's deliberately choose our mentors, surround ourselves with great company, go to museums, and read excellent books. As Joseph Campbell wrote, "All of life is a meditation. Most of it unintentional."

With that in mind, envision the qualities you would like to embody. Account for your free time: What small changes can you make to bring you closer to the person you wish to become? Who do you wish to study under in terms of books and lectures and discussions? You can pick anyone from history who left a paper trail.

The days of artists guilds are long gone, but the principle of copying, stealing, sampling, borrowing, and emulating from every good source allows us to follow in their footsteps. And take the words of John Ruskin to heart, "To study one good master till you understand him will teach you more than a superficial acquaintance with a thousand."

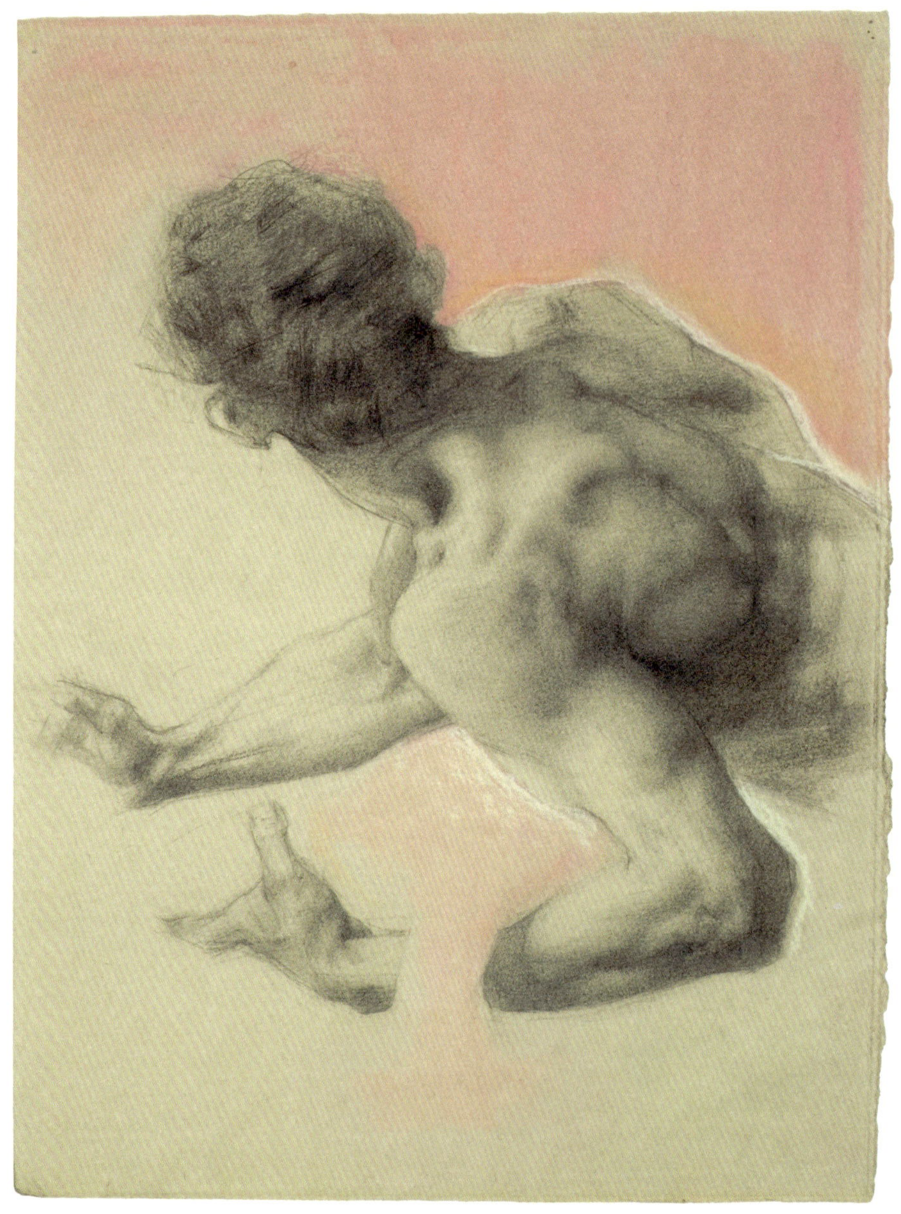

MASTERCOPY WORK

THE GREATEST ART in the world was produced from a system of learning from direct experience: apprenticing under a master. That model allowed for incremental growth, and students learned by doing. Complex tasks were broken down into smaller goals and tackled in a progression of increasing mastery. You learn to grind paint, transfer drawings, lay in underpaintings, and paint background elements. Geniuses followed the same path as everyone else. At age fifteen, Leonardo da Vinci was apprenticed to Andrea del Verrocchio, and he stayed for seven years. (The average time a student studied with a master was twelve years.) And so da Vinci learned every aspect of his craft and likewise artists across the centuries.

The practice of copying as an educational tool continued through the nineteenth century, as students drew from prints, engravings, casts, and sculptures before working from life. Students copied paintings until they were well advanced in their training. There were two main ways to make copies: stroke for stroke replicating of the painting and process as closely as possible or as an interpretation focusing on one aspect of the work for imitation.

Many artists continued this practice of sketching from works that inspired them in some form throughout their whole lives. This way of learning shaped the greatest artists the world has ever seen. And, can, still, for those that follow. This process of gradual mastery is still practiced within modern Atelier Programs.

On the opposite page is is my mastercopy of a Paul Baudry drawing. As artists, we often look back and create something new.

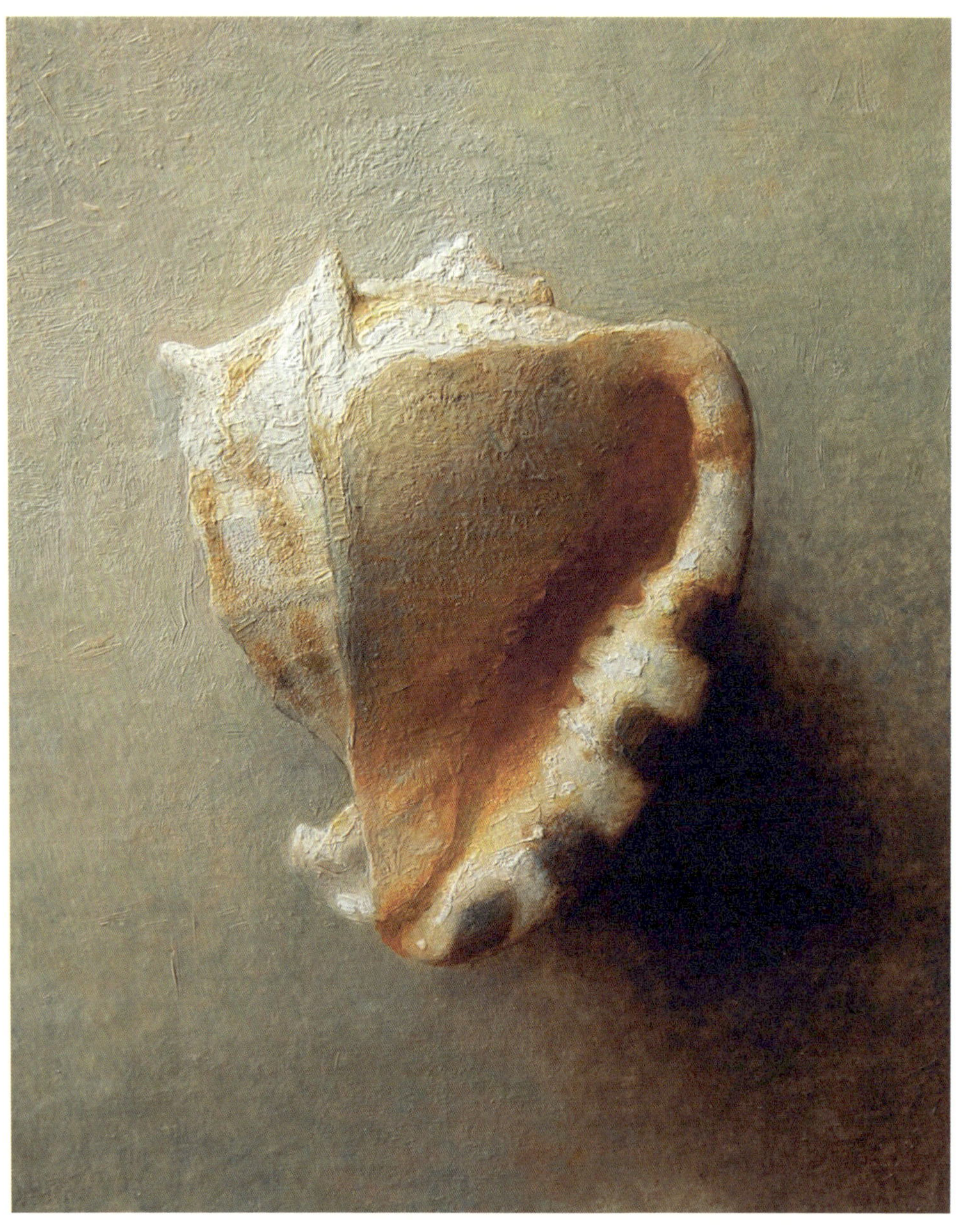

YOU ONLY NEED A PENCIL AND PAPER to dip into the historical practice of learning from master artists. Try it for yourself by sketching this shell by Charles Weed.

Start with a simple triangular outline working from larger shapes to smaller ones before putting in tone. You can spend a few minutes or come back time and again to add improvements. Any amount of practice will expand your appreciation of the art and add to your skills.

To get detailed drawing instruction, see my book: *Beginning Drawing Atelier.*

NOW, SURPRISE YOURSELF by drawing from memory. The 19th-century teacher Horace Lecoq de Boisbaudran trained artists diverse as Rodin and Alphonse Legros (art on p. 11). He sent them to the Louvre and then had them recreate the art work from memory in their studio.

Here, Artist Deborah Paris has adapted this practice for us:

- Let your eyes flow over the shell for a few minutes noticing what catches your attention. Close your eyes and imagine the image in your mind's eye.
- Now, cover the shell with a piece of paper and begin your drawing. Don't worry about mistakes. Stop when you feel your memory is exhausted.
- Rest for a few minutes. Look at the shell again for qualities like width to height, which way the shadow falls, and notice any strong angles. Cover the reference and continue to make corrections to your work.
- Later in the day, try the exercise again. Is it easier the second time and do you remember more?

170

[illegible] i [illegible] [illegible]
[illegible] na [illegible] [illegible] nie [illegible]
[illegible] i [illegible] [illegible] [illegible] się
więcej nie [illegible]. [illegible] [illegible]
[illegible] —

The way to love anything
is to realize
that it might be lost.
If you want to realize
the splendid vision
of all visible things,
wink the other eye.

—G.K. CHESTERTON

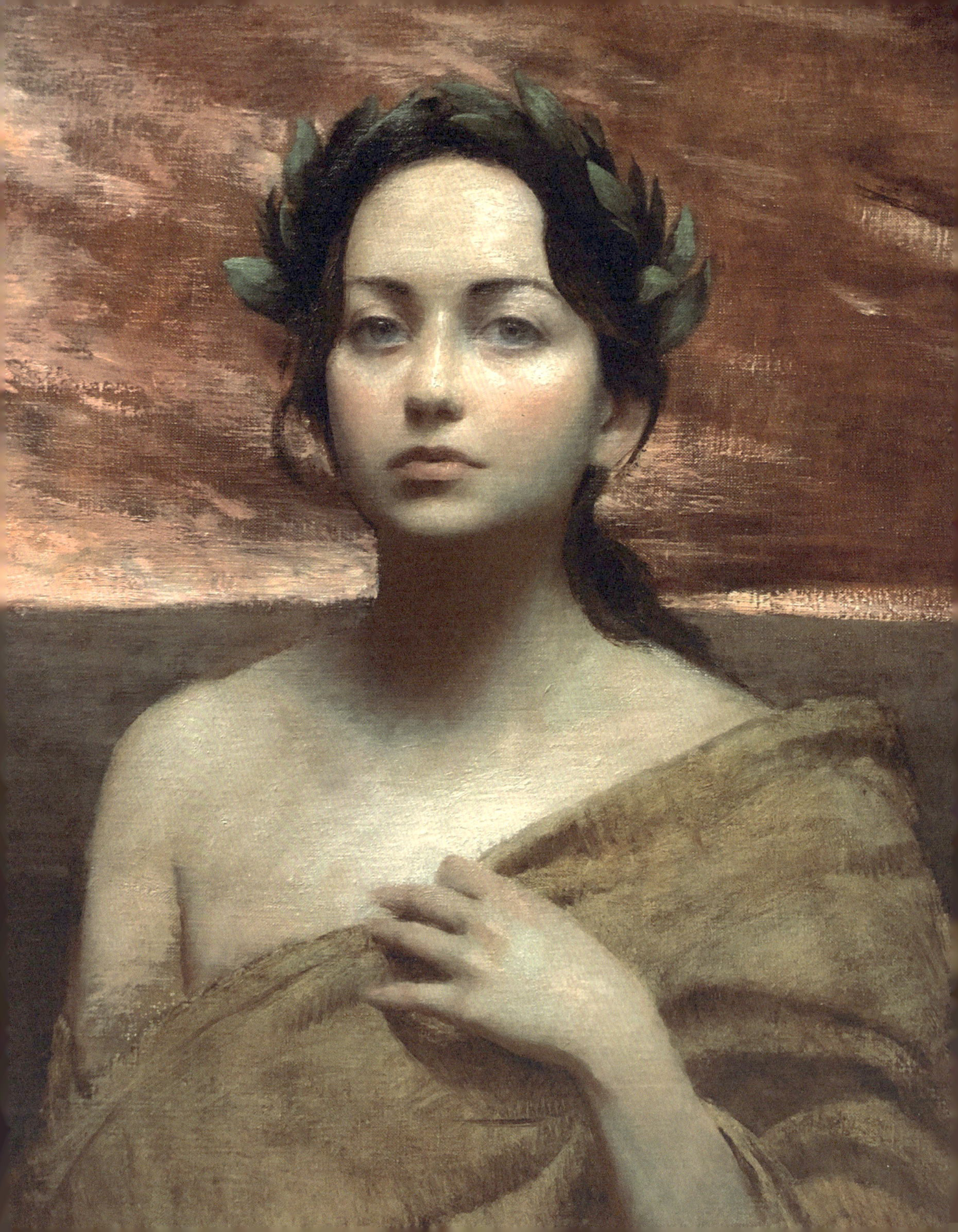

MIND THE GAP

There is such an interval between my ideal
and the actual in many instances
that I may say I am unborn.
—HENRY DAVID THOREAU

CLOSE YOUR EYES AND IMAGINE a single tree. What does your tree look like? Perhaps draw it on paper. Your tree, pulled from the ether of your mind, is a simplification, capturing universal attributes of all trees—much like the word *tree* stands as a pictograph of sorts in written or spoken language. We know in reality there are tens of thousands of types of trees and trillions of real ones. Anything with a name can be symbolized by its essential qualities.

Plato considered the unchanging archetype in the inner eye more real than what we actually see. The ideal exists only in the imagination, yet exerts a pull on our perception. Its tantalizing reach is explored frequently in art.

The ideal in art is a search for perfection. In ancient civilizations a thousand years of carvings conform so closely to a pattern that it can look like the work of one artisan. Dynastic cultures valued the eternal and changeless over the expressive and personal. In medieval iconography, saints are constructed from compass swings using the mind's eye rather than the optic nerve. It turns out that

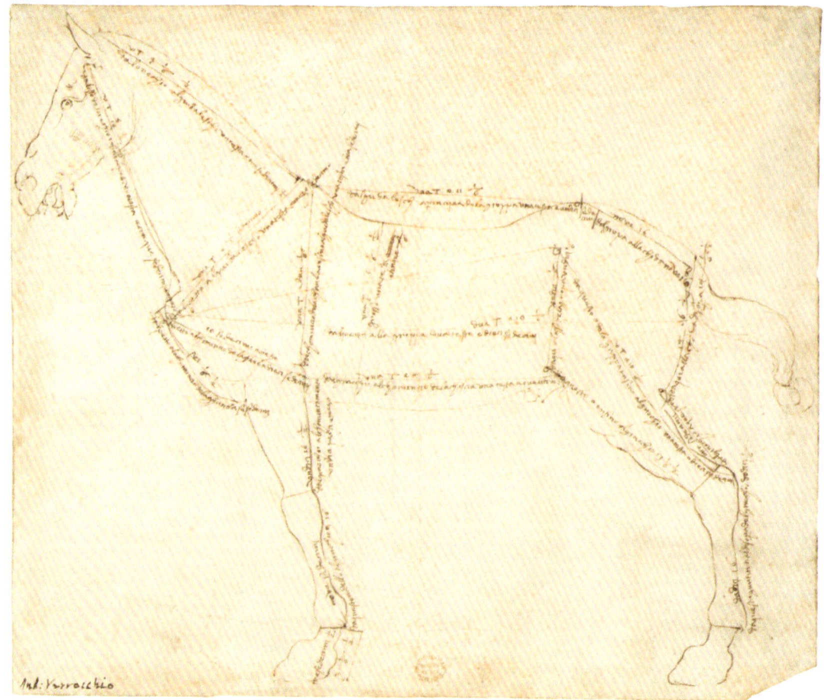

making art based on direct observation of nature happens only periodically in art history.

Renaissance artists searched for universal proportions with the same rigor that they studied visible nature. Patterns are discernible in all areas of life; they flicker and point to an order beneath a surface of unceasing change and chance. We still look for patterns because, after all, we are meaning-making beings.

I visited the Convent of San Marco and noticed that the inner courtyard was a tangled mass of wispy scrub and wildflowers. A curious choice in an otherwise curated environment. I climbed to the second floor and looked down from a window. The difference was so striking it took me a minute to register that I was seeing the exact same courtyard. Viewed from above, the tangle of flowers took on a clear organization. There was no confusion, only a tight geometric pattern—yet the only real change was my perspective. I would have never seen the underlying meaning at eye level and using my senses alone. It required intervention: in this case, a set of stairs.

Renaissance artists balanced a schema of inherited knowledge with careful observation of nature. They anticipated the model posing for a Madonna would be 7.5 heads high and chose to make her 8 heads high for grace or 7.25 heads high for accuracy to nature. They studied the nature of things, looking under the surface for the hand of God. Unlike medieval artists, Renaissance artists went directly to nature. Geometry provided a blueprint but nature had the last word.

When drawing from any living model, be it tree or person, we can look for these proportional systems, and real life will nod to our expectations and then happily do its own thing. Only by using what we know and see together do we do justice to the subject. When beginners draw from life or photos their drawings are often misshapen until they learn to find the structure.

Patterns are only recognized by comparison and when seen from a distance. Close up, all we have is the personal. Today, we have lost our taste for perfect forms and overarching cultural ideals. Many narratives and stories seem intrusive and out of touch as they fail to take into account our uniqueness and individuality. The Japanese aesthetic of *wabi-sabi* feels truer to our times based on its acceptance of transience and the faded and worn.

Imperfection is in some sort essential
to all that we know of life. . .
that neither architecture
nor any other noble work of man
can be good
unless it be imperfect.

—JOHN RUSKIN

Between the real and the ideal is a gap, and it can be a painful one. Yet, it's only when someone gets close enough to see the worry lines, to spot the sorrow, that they are close enough to love you. The mask is down. We may deeply admire those we worship from a distance, but real love is harder won. To see someone as perfect means keeping them at arm's length; the only way to stay an ideal is not to be known.

Yet, perfection is not so easily dismissed. It can spur us on to achievement and point to something beyond us worth striving for. It can also inspire us to higher goals and to virtue. When we see a glimmer of the ideal in a broken person, it can help us respect the divine qualities within them. In times of flux and tumult, the ideal can remind us that there is more to life than what we see with our eyes.

Every artist feels the pull more toward the ideal or real based on their temperament and aesthetic. The artistic process reconciles those extremes through working from general to specific. After all, the portrait artist doesn't start with the eyelashes but rather the broadest strokes of the head. Yet when finishing, no detail is too small. All art falls somewhere on the spectrum of extremes, reconciled through the person of the artist.

I was on the NYC subway on my way to teach a workshop. The lesson I had planned was on proportion and measurement. I mused

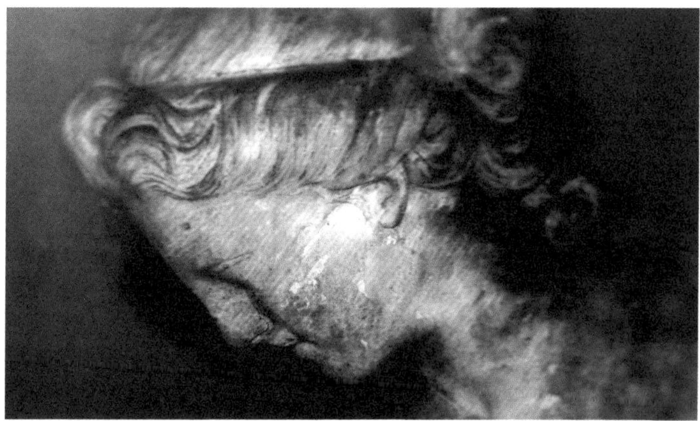

on how to present this tension between the real and ideal in great drawing. Looking up, I noticed a poem just above the heads of the people across from me. (Thank you NYC Transit Authority!)

I had plenty of time to ponder this poem by Charles Reznikoff:

> If there is a scheme,
> perhaps this too is in the scheme,
> as when a subway car turns on a switch,
> the wheels screeching against the rails,
> and the lights go out—
> but are on again in a moment.

I've lived long enough now to love the plan and hope that all goes according to it. Yet, when the lights go out and the car screeches, life can go off the rails. We are forged in those moments off the tracks. The reality of being alive is that life rarely follows the plan in the way we expect. Art, mirroring life, toggles between the ideal we strive for and the reality we see. Remember that everything looks perfect from far away, and when trying to get close, please remember to mind the gap.

FINDING THE STRUCTURE OF A FACE

THE STRUCTURE OF THE HUMAN FACE is consistent across time, age, gender and culture. This pattern provides a hidden order that underlies our unique features. Artists look for this proportional cannon, to create a feeling of strength and stability under a surface of continual change.

Can you find an element of structure of a face like a master artist? In Rubens' sketchbook he explored the triangular relationship between the eyes, nose and ears of a face. Can you see the triangle in the sculpture of the Roman bust? Now, look at yourself in the mirror or at a friend until you see those same relationships. You have caught a glimpse of a divine scaffolding.

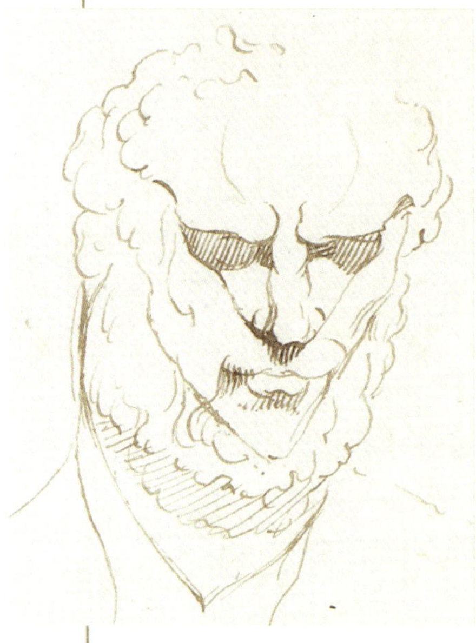

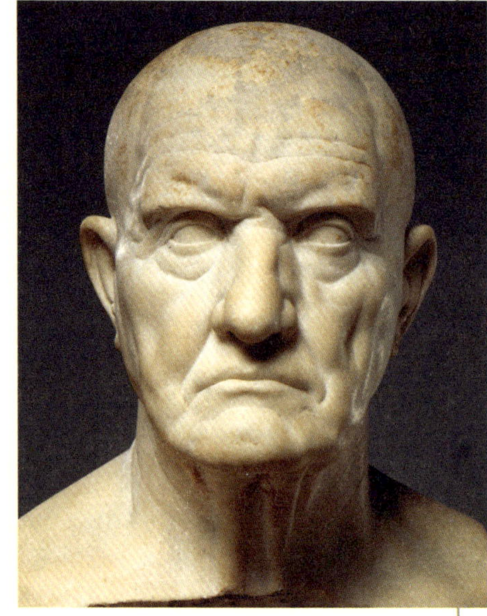

WHO IS MORE PERFECT?

HOW DOES THE PERFECTION of a disposable cup compare to the imperfection of a clay handmade one? Is a lumpy, yellow heirloom tomato less perfect than the red-sphere grocery store tomato? Is your homemade bread, full of irregularities, less ideal than the uniform rectangle of a store-bought loaf? Compare the old and young woman, who is more perfect? Why?

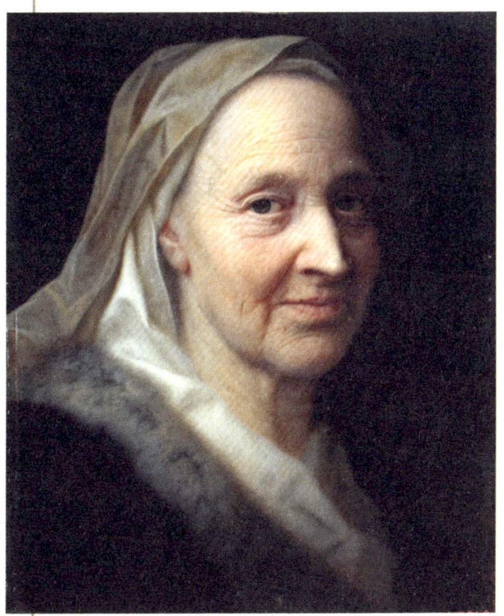

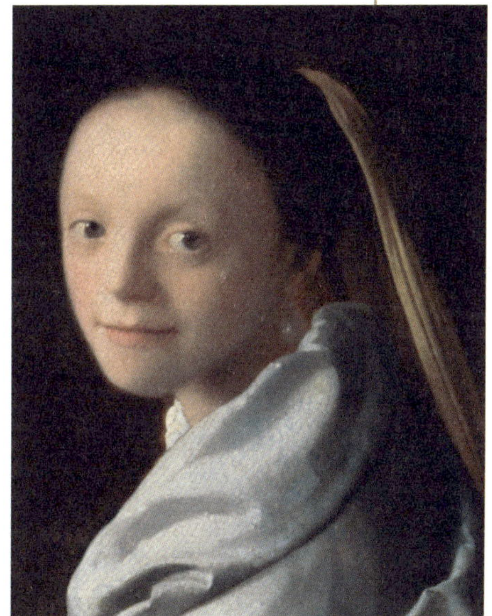

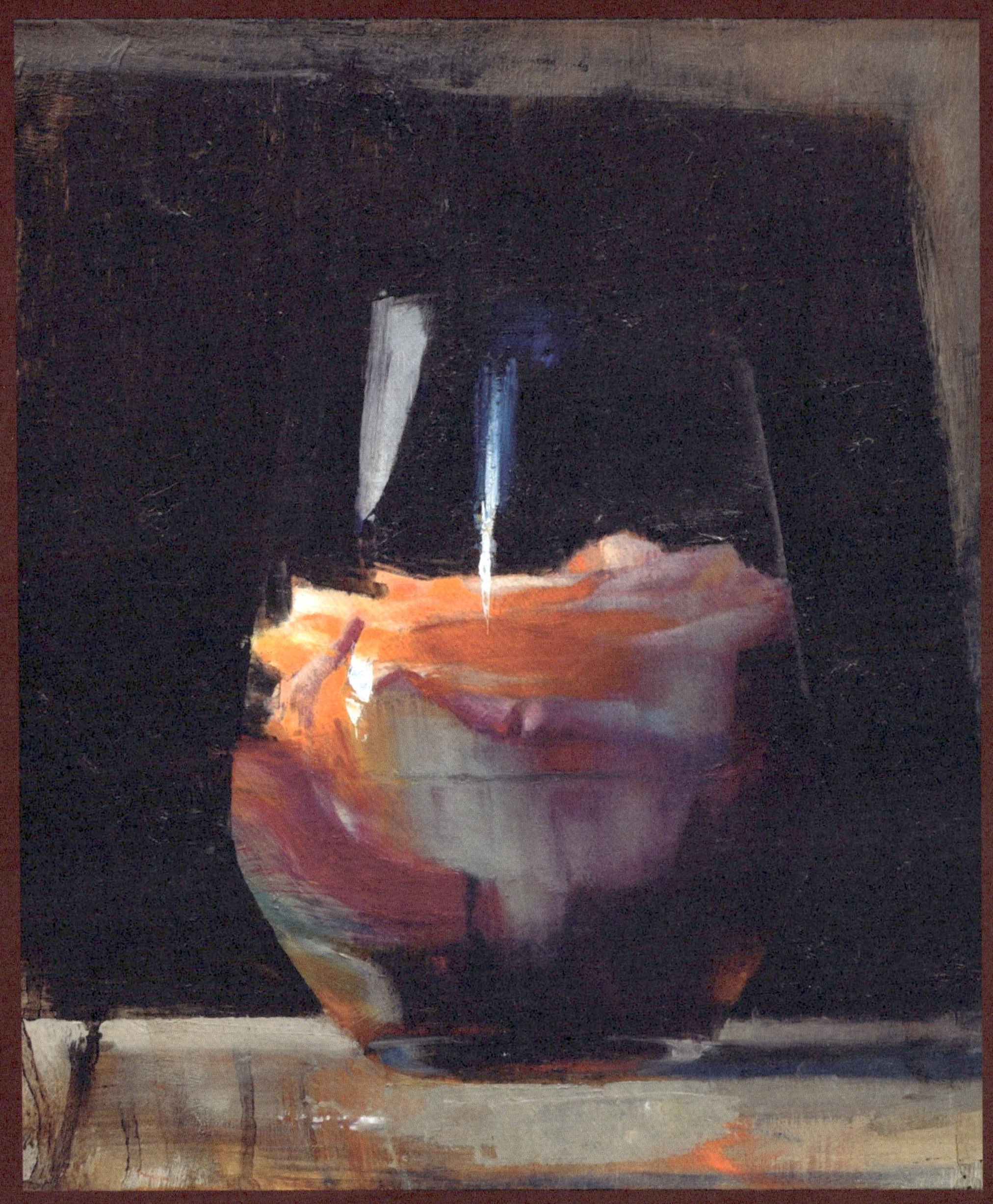

The way you look at things
is the most powerful force
in shaping your life.
In a vital sense,
perception is reality.

—JOHN O'DONOGHUE

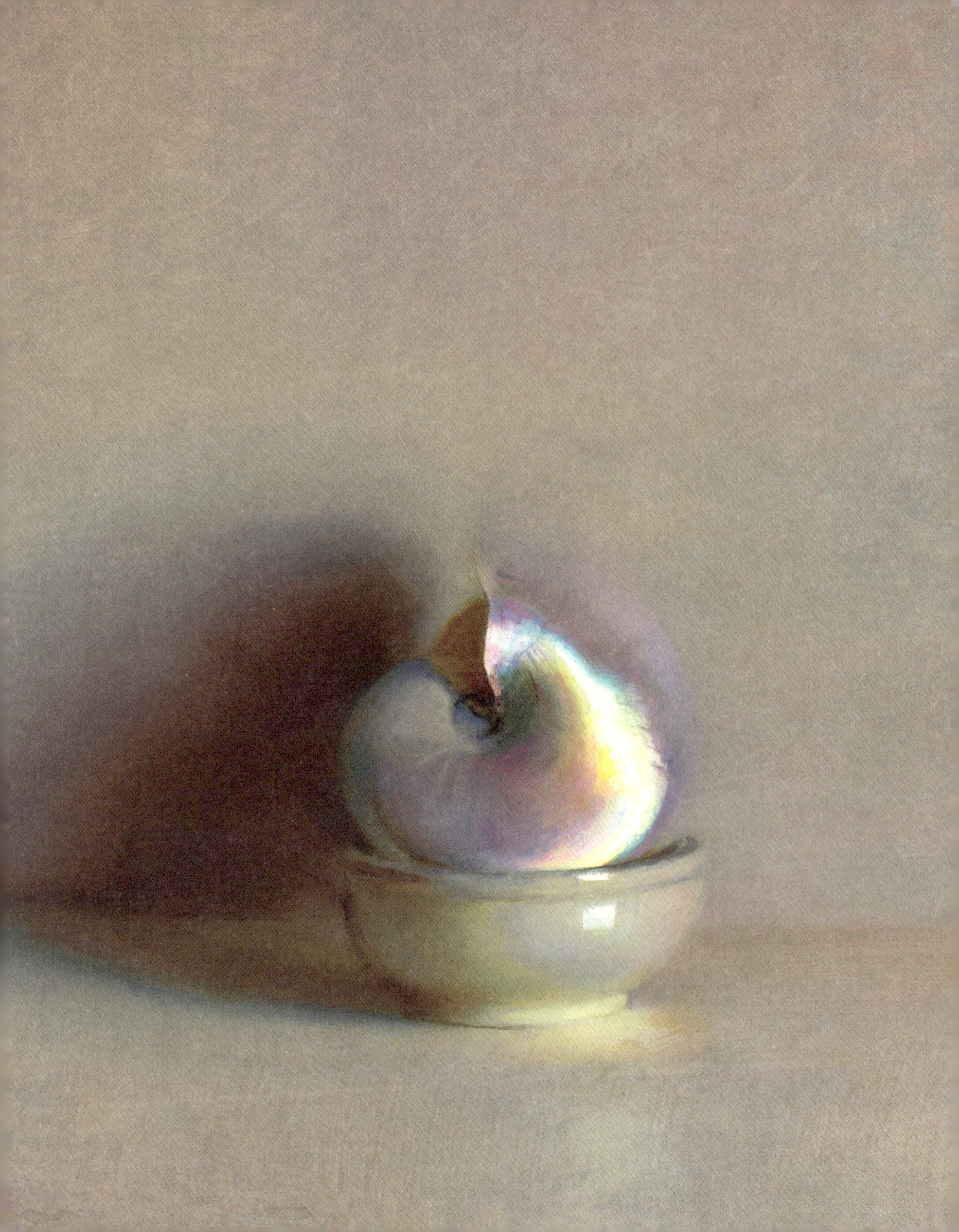

ART
OF ILLUSION

The question is not what you look at,
but what you see.

—HENRY DAVID THOREAU

GOING TO THE WOODS is a habit of mine in stressful times. One day I took a walk along the bottom of a tree-lined ravine where a stream rippled past a bank of watercress. The woods were serene, so I sat down to linger. Suddenly there was a terrific crash like cannon fire exploding without warning. A strong wind rushed across the ravine, knocking branches off the tree canopy high above. I sprinted up the hill to my car, my heart pounding through my chest, hoping not to get hit by falling limbs.

The next day, I asked my coworker Carol for advice about a particular problem. She told me to remember that things will work out and a tree falling in the forest makes more sound than an entire forest growing. It was eerily fitting. Carol was right in her observation (though I think she undersold the point): a tree falling in the forest makes infinitely more sound than a forest growing; it eclipses it entirely. And yet, while it's loud, it isn't the whole story. The forest I thought was collapsing is still a thriving ecosystem; the few downed branches were an anomaly.

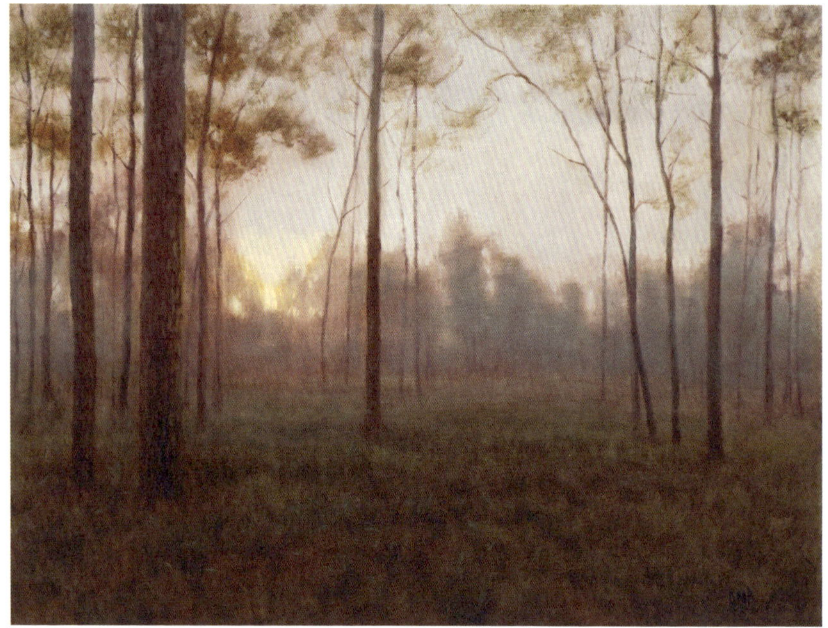

It is human nature, my nature, to focus on the negative. If we fix our eyes on these disasters, they eclipse beauty and goodness. The most shocking and upsetting things have the power to arrest our attention as a moon is eclipsed by my thumb. In art terms that is the area of highest contrast, yet complexity and subtlety only happen within art and life, in shades of gray.

So, let's distinguish between what calls for our notice and what deserves our notice. Human sight is changeable, subjective, and influenced by variables so complex that two people can look at the same thing and see something entirely different; even within ourselves, perspective can change from minute to minute. We have enormous power to shape what we see because meaning and attention are not fixed, but malleable. How we see affects *what* we see, and beauty, like little else, shines a mirror on our own capacity.

FOREGROUND AND BACKGROUND

Negative space in art is the area between and around an object that has its own presence and purpose. In drawing and painting, we focus on the forms that project toward us. Yet in life, a building is made by the spaces it envelops, and our open squares designate an invitation to gather, just as the pauses between notes create music. The likeness of a person, wrote John Berger, is the space that they leave behind when they pass. This painting by Gary Faigin plays with our ideas of foreground and background through his use of negative space. Can you find the still life objects in this painting?

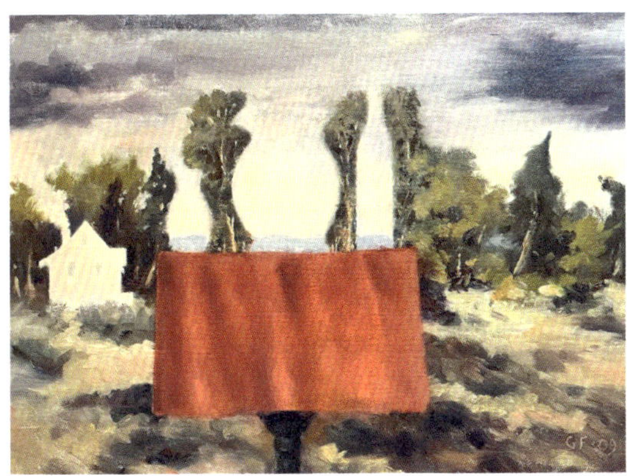

PERCEPTION AS ACTION

Jason Barton, a neuro-ophthalmologist and a visual neuroscientist at the University of British Columbia, joined us in the Atelier to answer the question: "How do we see?" Although the immediate answer may be, "with our eyes," it is the brain that interprets the flashes of light the eye sees to make sense of our visual world. Think of perception as a dance between vision, attention, and eye movements. So, while seeing is natural, perception isn't passive.

What calls or grabs our attention? Certain properties draw us; high contrast, bright colors, flicker, or movement—examples of *salience*. It is hard not to look at something that suddenly appears or starts to move.

However, salience is only one factor that determines where we look. *Relevance* is what is personally important to us. We all have different interests and experiences and we focus on different things even when we are looking at the same image. So, a car buff and an architect will perceive an urban street scene differently.

PERCEPTION AND THE ARTIST

While perception is an active goal-directed process, the artist can steer that process through knowledge of salience and relevance. These powerful tools can either strengthen or detract from our message based on how we use them. Whether abstract or representational, artworks create narratives, provoke emotions, generate conflicts, and raise questions. How we look at something is important. And if we don't pay attention to something, we might as well not have seen it.

People look at art longer than they do objects in life. Why? Our perceptual system is being challenged by subtleties in the work. We linger over images that raise questions, that have ambiguity, or create a paradox. You could let these things happen by chance, but mastery controls the message. When making a painting, you should ask: Where do you want the focal point to be, and why?

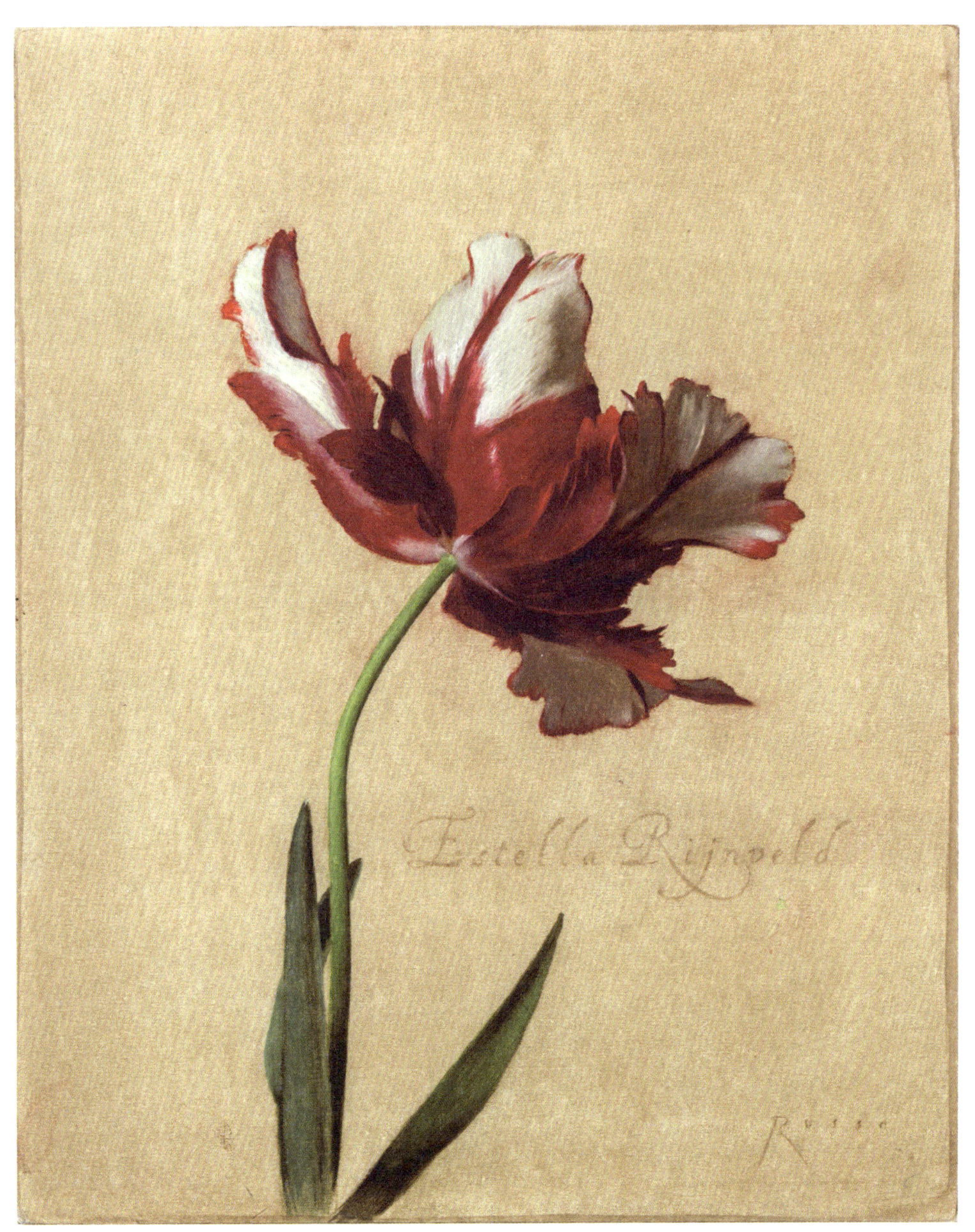
Estella Rijnveld

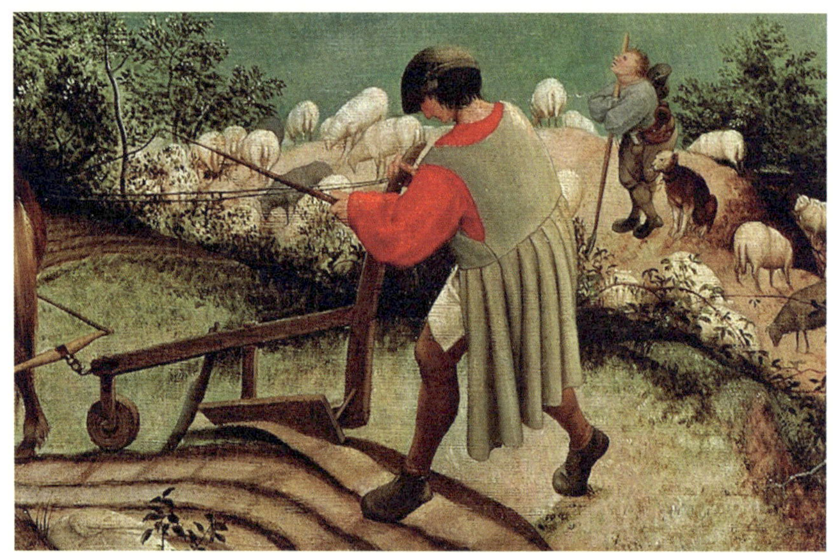

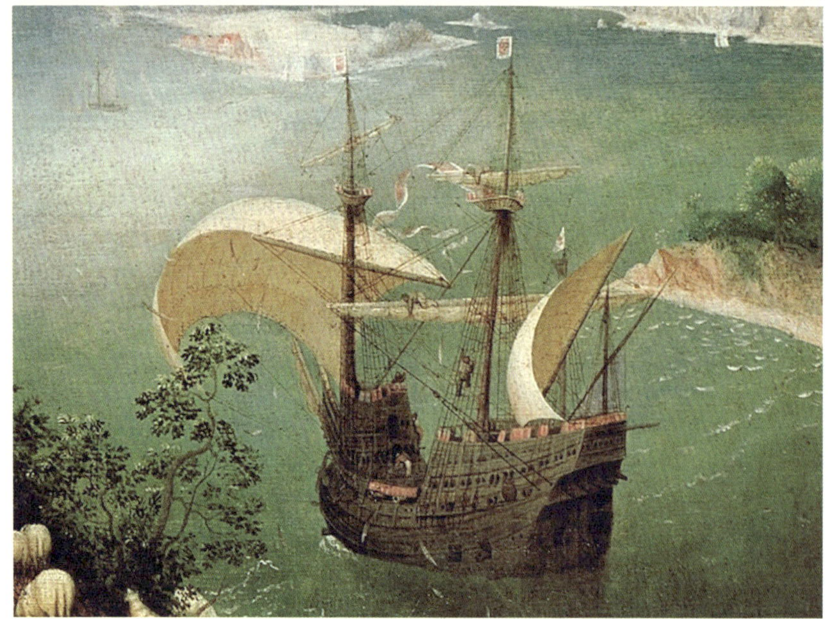

WHAT DO YOU SEE?

WHAT DO YOU THINK is the subject of this painting? If you had to give this work a title, what name might you suggest?

ATTENTION is like a spotlight that can only shine one thing at time. To test this premise, look at the image and try to concentrate on both the man and the ship.

Look at the painting again. The unlikely title for the work is *Landscape with the Fall of Icarus* by Bruegel the Elder. Now that you know its name, where do your eyes focus and does that change the meaning of the piece? Consider that when we look at our world, we see with clarity *either*: the man *or* the ship, the grand scope or the detail, the exploding tree or the forest growing.

IF YOU WISH, look up W. H. Auden's "Musée des Beaux Arts" for an example of a famous ekphrastic poem about this painting.

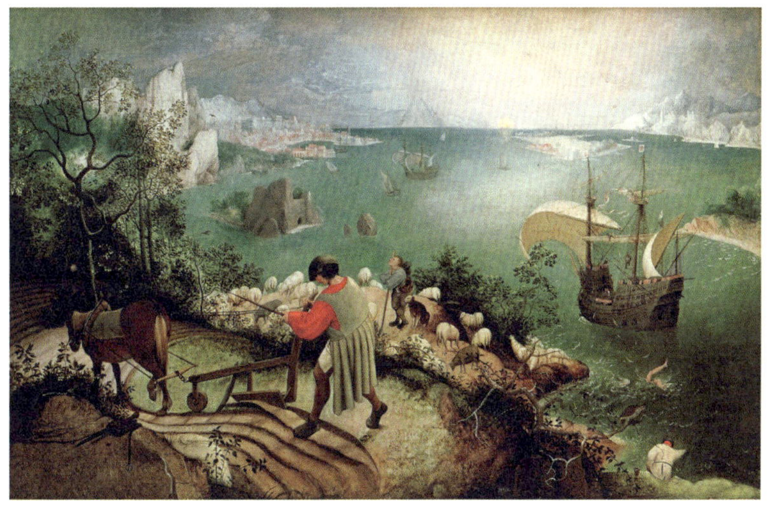

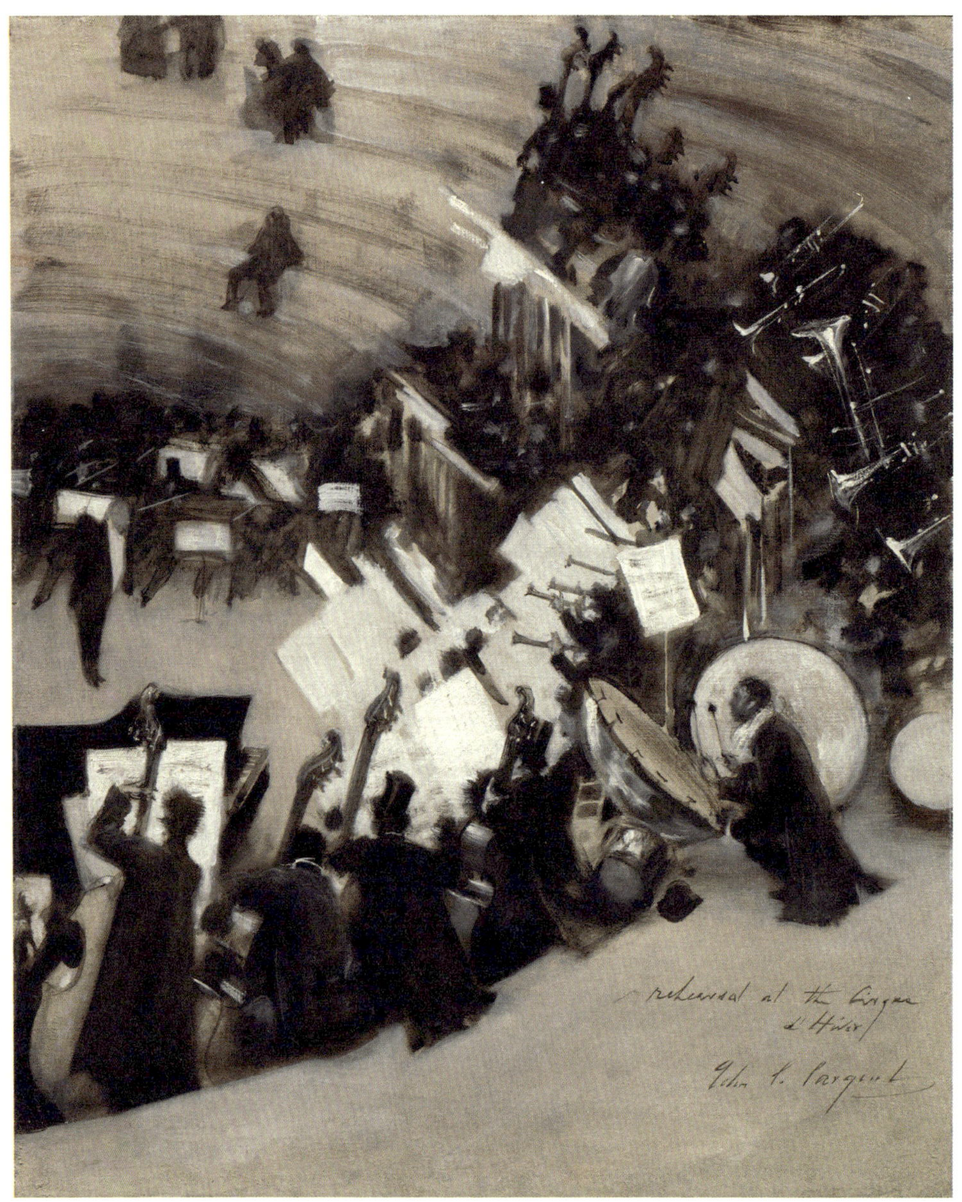

SEE ART LIKE A NEUROSCIENTIST

DR. JASON BARTON LEADS US through an analysis of John Singer Sargent's *Rehearsal of the Pasdeloup Orchestra* (opposite). Vision is a goal-directed process requiring the eye and brain to work together to allocate attention and ascribe meaning. Seeing requires a combination of eye movements, salience, and relevance.

Salience is the property that makes something stand out. A high contrast of color or value, or a moment that pulls our eye. Relevance is equally important. Does something have social or personal significance to us? If so, that will direct our vision in art, as in life.

LOOKING AT THE IMAGE, locate the areas of salience:

- What are the brightest regions with the greatest contrast which grab our attention?

WHAT ABOUT RELEVANCE?

- What is happening in the picture that would cause us to look in a particular spot?

Once salience has drawn us to look at the musicians, we realize that their gaze and their instruments are pointing towards a location to the mid-left of the image. If we have already read the title of the work, we understand this is an orchestra in rehearsal, so the person the musicians are looking at must be the conductor (possibly Jules-Étienne Pasdeloup himself).

Both of these points of social relevance direct us to the shadowy figure in the mid-left location. The overall result is a picture with two areas of focus in tension with each other: a salient one where all the bright white sheet music lies, and a relevant one, where the conductor stands, creating a visual tension that flickers without settling.

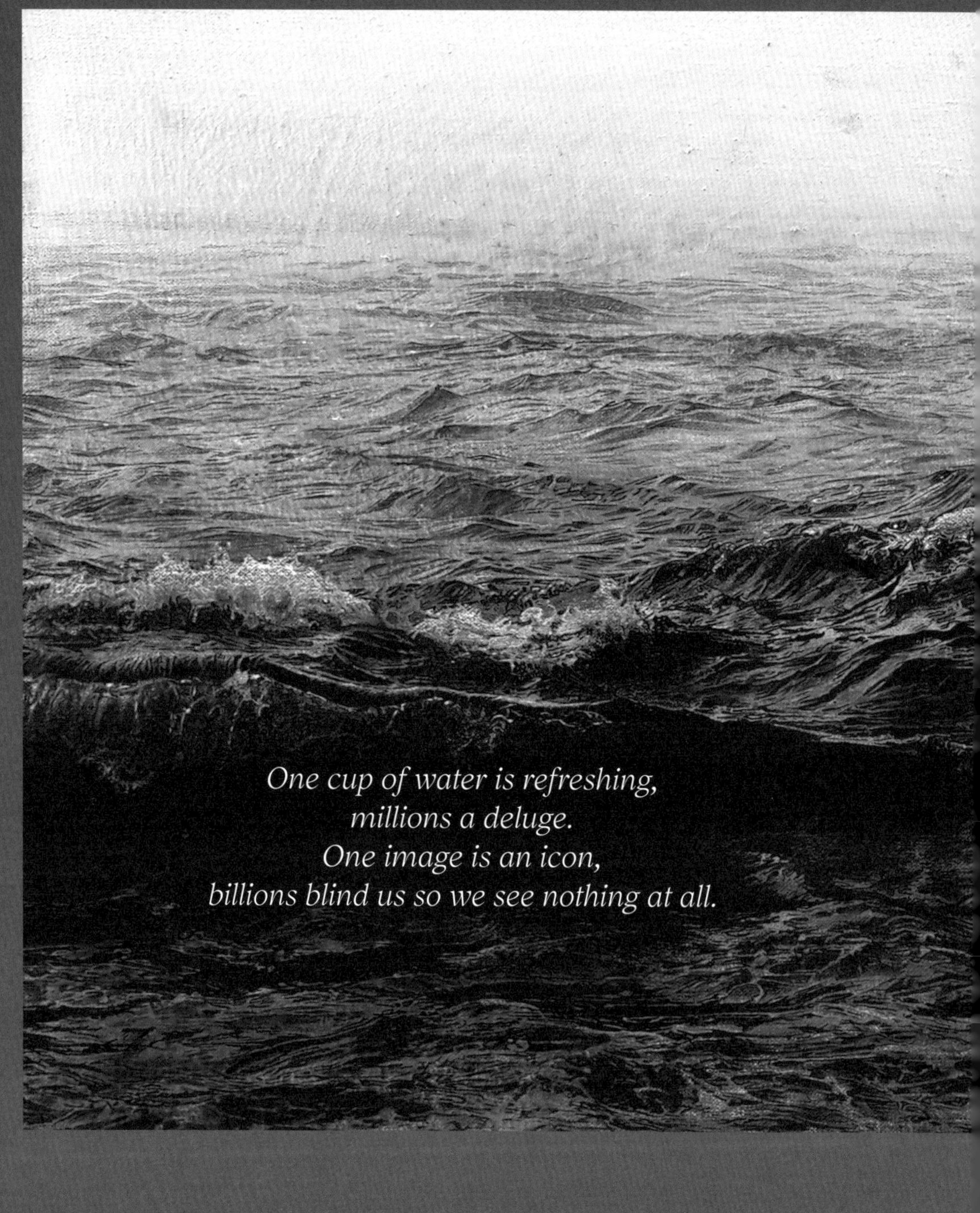

One cup of water is refreshing,
millions a deluge.
One image is an icon,
billions blind us so we see nothing at all.

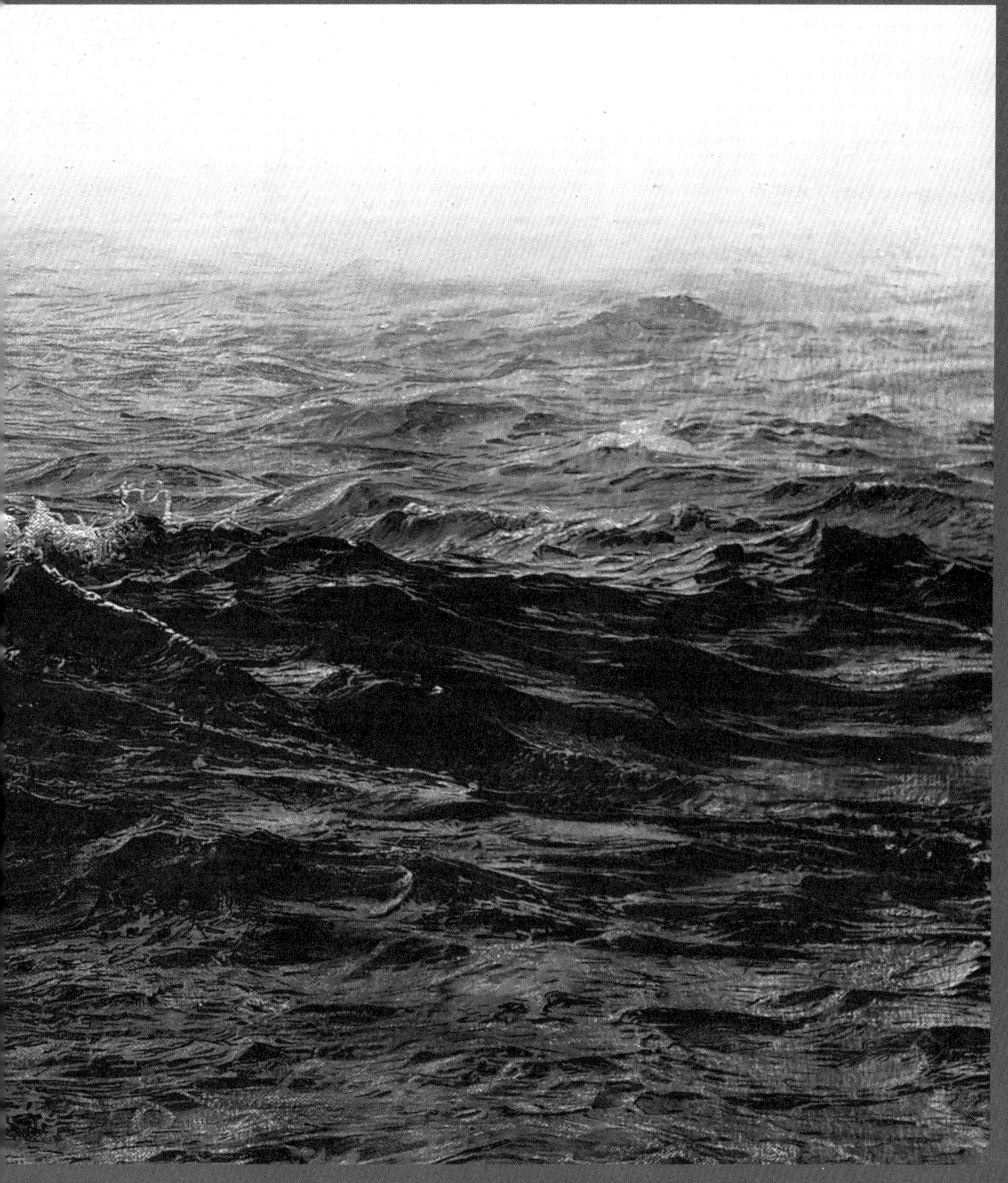

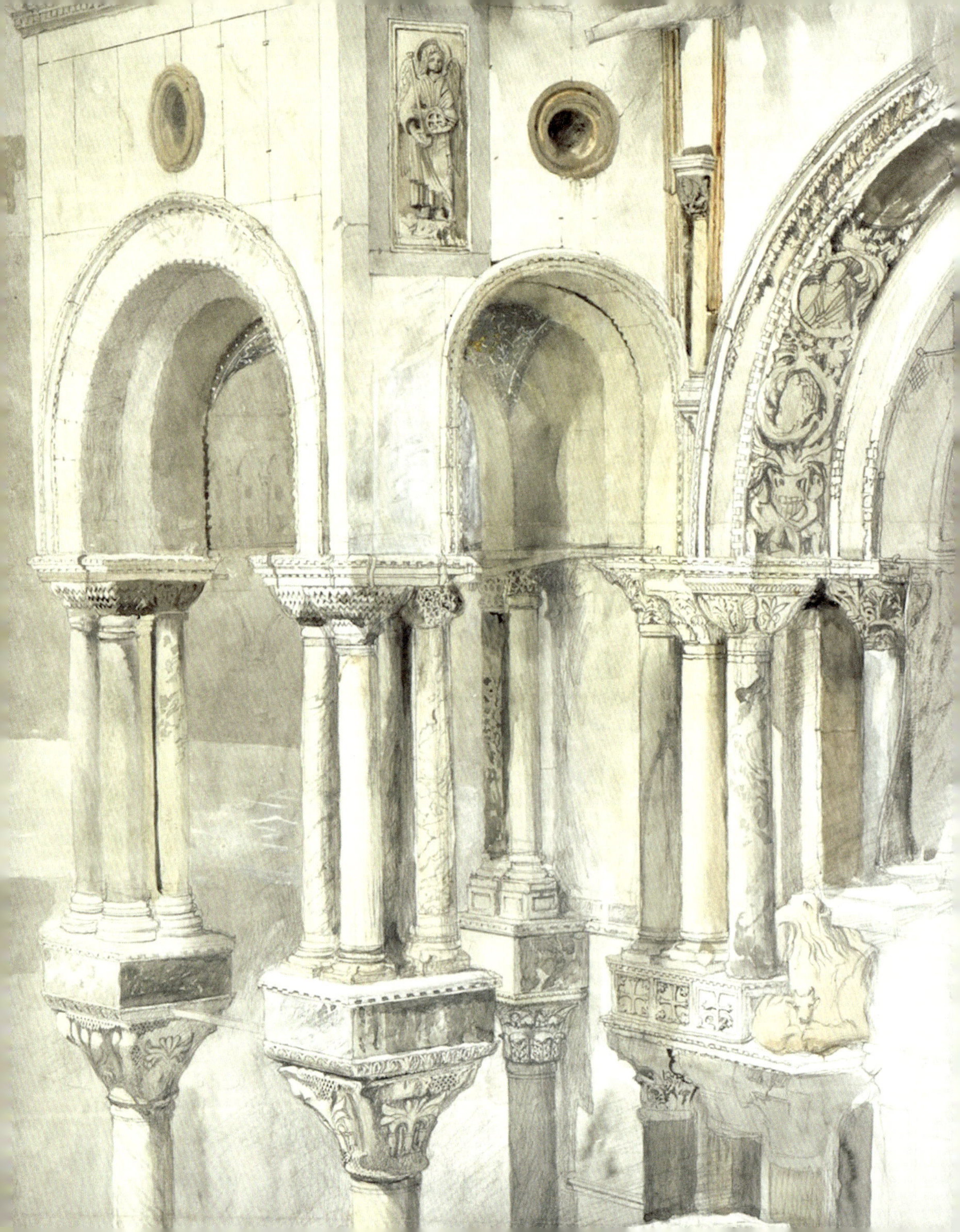

ARCHITECTURA

A building which is truly a work of art . . .
must have, almost literally, a life.
—LOUIS SULLIVAN

WHERE I LIVE, buildings are built to look like multiuse workspaces for evil geniuses: one part prison, one part chemical factory, and just a hint of nuclear bunker. My eyes are acclimated to frugal Pacific Northwest minimalism. In new construction every consideration is sublimated to utility. When I was in Florence this summer, I spent much time looking at the facade of Santa Croce deep in philosophical thought. Honestly, I was drinking my weight in cocktails, yet even in my blurry-brained state I could see the buildings are awe-inspiring. I'd have to be completely insensate to miss it.

In my neighborhood I would never sit in a square admiring the buildings; there are few beautiful buildings to speak of and no squares. I also have lived here so long that my senses are dulled by habit. It's a proof point for German philosopher Walter Benjamin's theory that architecture is a form of mass art consumed within a state of distraction—unless of course one is on vacation. And, with respect to utility, while many art forms come and go, architecture remains constant by necessity. We absorb our buildings into our consciousness through the act of living.

One warm evening, too tired to talk, a friend and I drew the entire Santa Croce facade in ten minutes as a dare. The ornamentation was so dazzling that I expected to do no more than mindlessly copy a bit of it. Yet with a pencil in hand, I worked methodically, from large shapes to small, running my angles and searching for repeatable relationships. To my surprise, the architecture subdivided with the satisfying measurements of an antique bust. I realized that, although I understand no Italian aside from *ciao*, I could understand the language of this building.

> *A Cathedral is built on the principle of living bodies. Its concordances, its equilibriums, exactly follow the general laws according to nature's order.*
>
> —AUGUSTE RODIN

Just as sonnets have fourteen lines, Western musicians use a seven-note scale, and chess has its eight-by-eight board, buildings designed by artists use consistent principles of design. In the time before specialization many buildings were designed by remarkable architects who were also artists. Titans such as Raphael, Michelangelo, Giotto, and many others used the simple divisions of musical harmony.* Noted art historian Rudolf Wittkower wrote that during the Renaissance, "Musical consonances were the audible tests of a universal harmony which had a binding force for all the arts." Design and composition have common fundamentals across vastly different forms.

*These principles were laid out by Leon Battista Alberti in his *Ten Books on Architecture*. My husband Constantine Aristides coined the term *harmonic* ratio to describe the armature of a rectangle that was in use during this time.

These beautiful buildings resonate with us because we sense something familiar about them, they are representations of ourselves. The classical principles of architecture were based on the human body. Mathematician Luca Pacioli, a friend of da Vinci, wrote that tucked within the human body are ratios and proportions of God's design which the ancients used in their architecture, especially their temples. He wrote, "For in the human body they (the ancients) found the two main figures without which it is impossible to achieve anything, namely the perfect circle and the square." The most famous illustration of this is da Vinci's *Vitruvian Man* where, when the arms of a person are outstretched, they fit into a square, and when all the limbs are extended they form a circle.

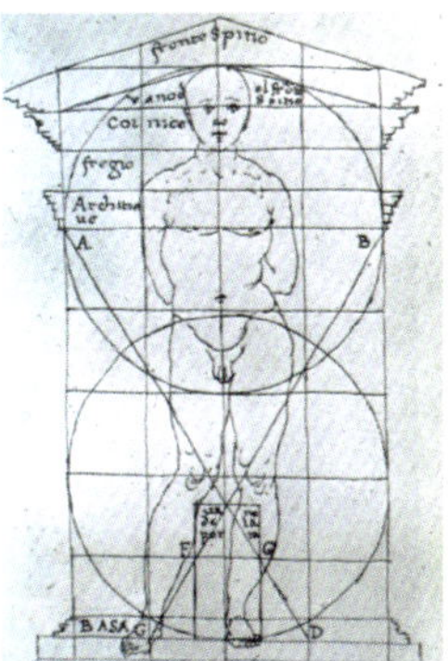

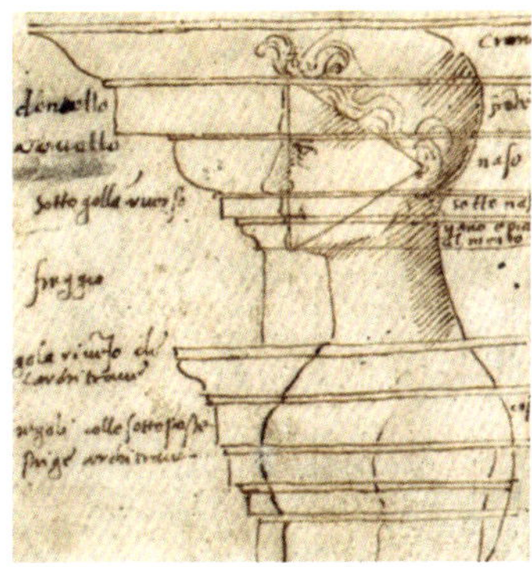

Artists are poised to understand architecture because we rigorously study the human body in our life drawing and anatomy classes. The bony landmarks of the figure are constant across race, gender, and age; a consistent unit of measurement is locked into our own skeletons. Such as, the width and height of the ball of the cranium (the parietal eminence) are the same size as the sternum, which is the same length as the clavicle, its width the height of the scapula and twice that of the femur, and so on. Likewise, the elements of buildings relate to one another based on the proportions of a figure. Harmony exists where the parts are related to each other and to the whole in just proportion.

In ancient architecture, the figure is everywhere. The columns were designed to look like women, the entablature like a face, the floor plan like the whole figure. Using a system of squares, Renaissance architects and artists aimed for harmony in their art, the goals being threefold: structural integrity, functionality, and beauty.

The geometric shapes of the circle and square are found in nature and every culture on earth. The circle can be seen in increasing size through a drop of water, the orb of an eye, or the sphere of a planet. It's used as a mandala for meditation, forms a halo on a saint, or promises the enduring nature of love in a ring. A circle exhibits the perfect unity of God, one without beginning or end, and is both here (a single point) and everywhere (infinite points). The circle nods to the cycle of growth and of seasons, the span of time in the days, months, and years. Through this loop we can see ourselves in this beautiful order of creation.

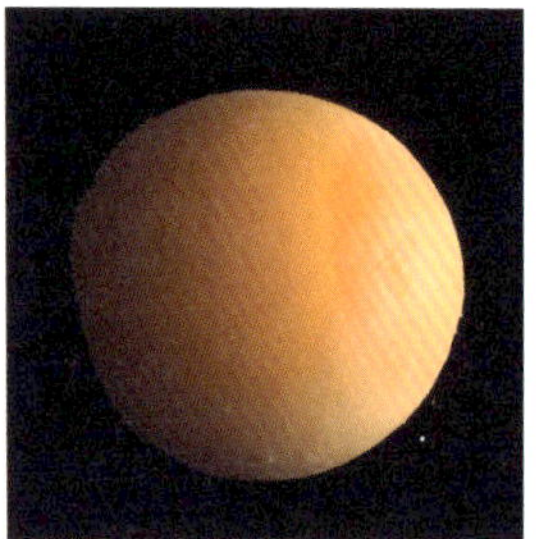

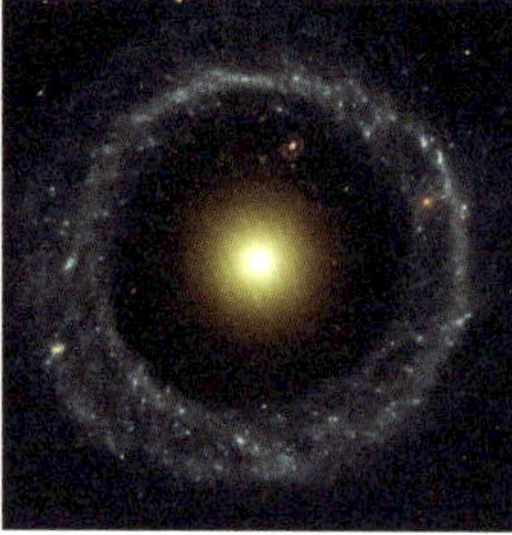

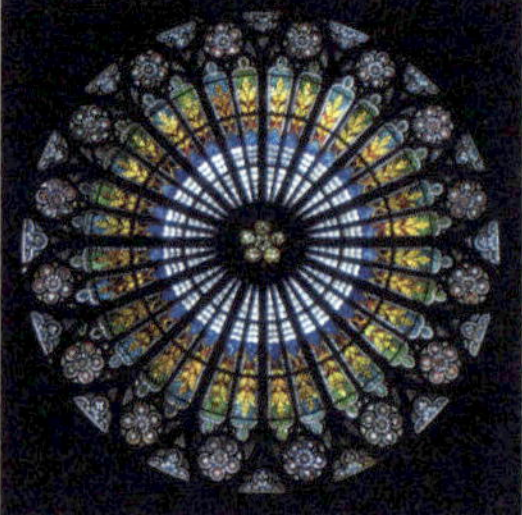

As small as an egg or as large as a galaxy

Where the circle points to the divine, the square describes the earthly with its stable foundation—the legs of a chair, the lintels of a doorway or window. The straight, equal sides denote the finite rationality of a human intelligence. This unit is found wherever people build and measure. It implies the human-made, seen in the shapes of our houses and also in the scoring of fields.

Architecture affects our state of mind, sending us messages about ourselves. I've experienced the frustration of walking through an innovative new library which accidentally fed me into a stairwell when I was trying to find the art section. The building seemed to say, "you are not welcome here." By contrast, the first time I went into San Marco Monastery in Florence I was filled with awe. Designed by the Medici architect Michelozzo, the beauty of its spaces brought out the highest version of myself. The interior spoke about communal life while valuing the solitary pursuits of study and prayer.

Too many places feel architecturally transient and alienating. Although we create our spaces, they, in turn, create us. What do these public and private spaces tell us about ourselves and our communities?

My Atelier students visited the Frye Art Museum years ago with the assignment to write down how the space spoke to them. By complete coincidence, the architect's son was in that class and he confirmed many of the things we suspected as attentive visitors.

The entrance to the museum was a gradual ramp next to a still pool of water under an awning. We are all equal; everyone, able-bodied or otherwise, takes the same way in. The pool leads us in a meditative, peaceful transition from the street to the interior. The awning lowers the amount of light hitting our eyes until they adjust to the light in the galleries. The doors are heavy, designed to look like an entrance to a vault, indicating something precious is inside. And through them, in the rotunda is a domed ceiling, a nod to the Pantheon Oculus highlighting the link between new and old.

We designed the entrance to the Atelier based on our experience of walking into this building. We strode a little taller when we stepped through the front door. It reminded us of who we wish to be.

Great architecture of the past was created in keeping with the principles of nature resulting in buildings that felt in harmony with the physical and spiritual life people who lived there. Beautiful design contributes to our happiness by showing that we belong. Ultimately, the most important role of a building is to house a daydreamer, along with their family and friends, so we can be alone together in the best sense of the word.

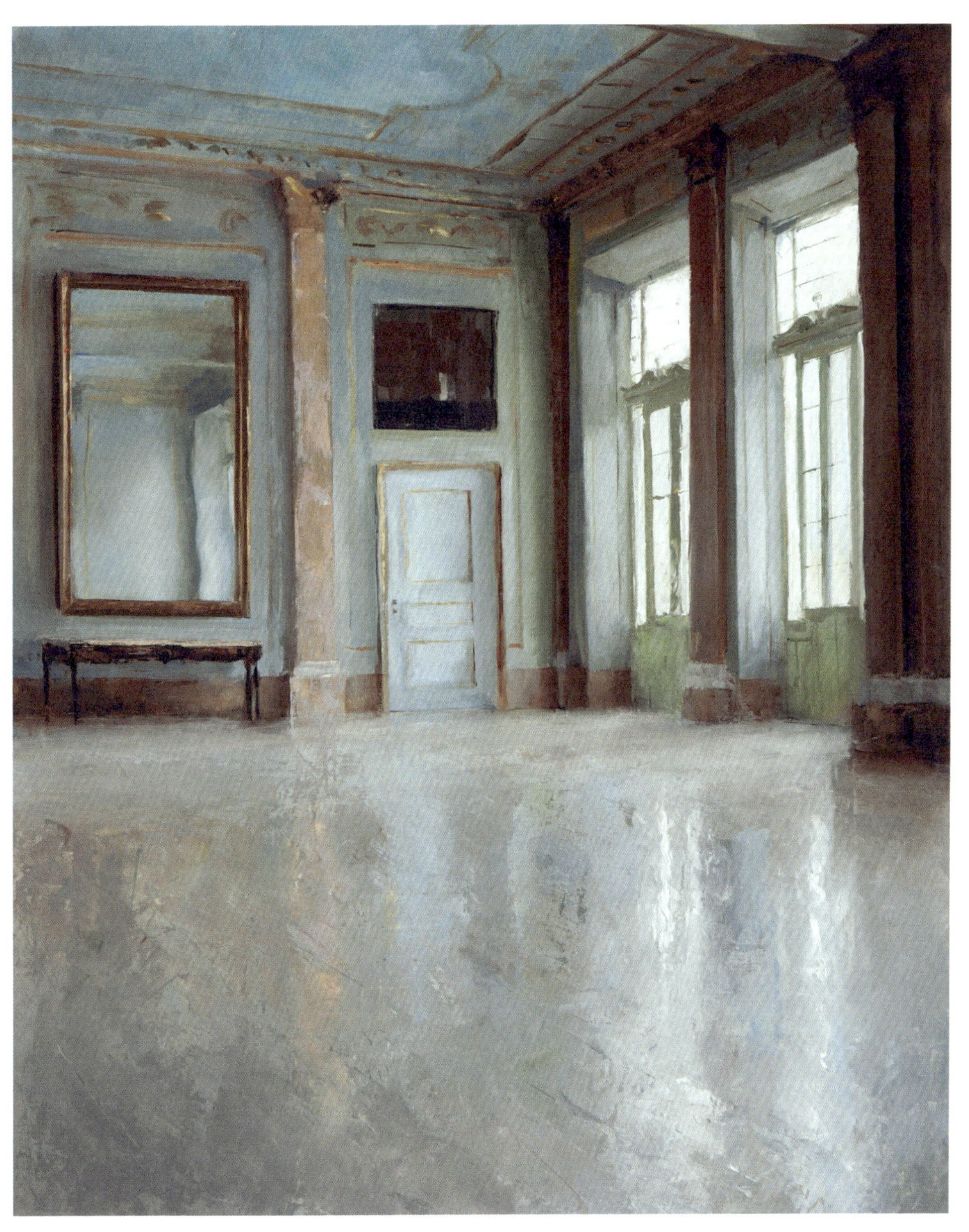

ARMATURE OF A SQUARE

THE BASIC DIVISIONS of a square are called an armature. By dividing the square into its diagonal and diamond shape, you can find the divisions of ½ or ⅓ and ⅔ easily without measuring. These are the same divisions that you will see throughout Renaissance paintings.

On a separate piece of paper, make the armature of a square to see how simple crossing lines divide the square. Start by making the X from the corners of a square to find the halfway marks, then find the large diamond shape. To locate the thirds, connect the corners with a V to the halfway mark on the sides.

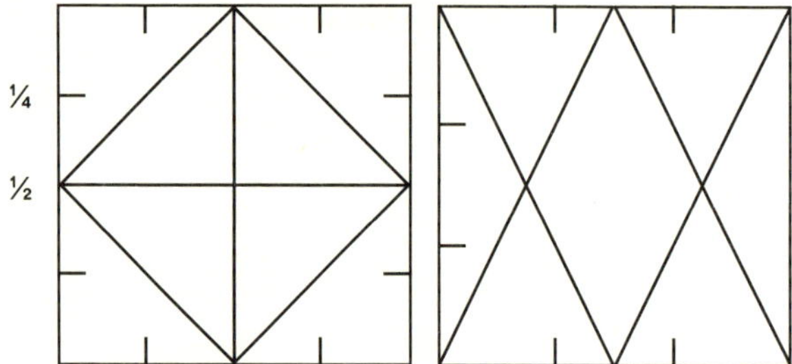

Now apply it to the facade of Santa Croce designed by architect Niccolò Matas. As an example, take a look at Rudolf Wittkower's analysis of Santa Maria Novella as a clue to get you started (below).

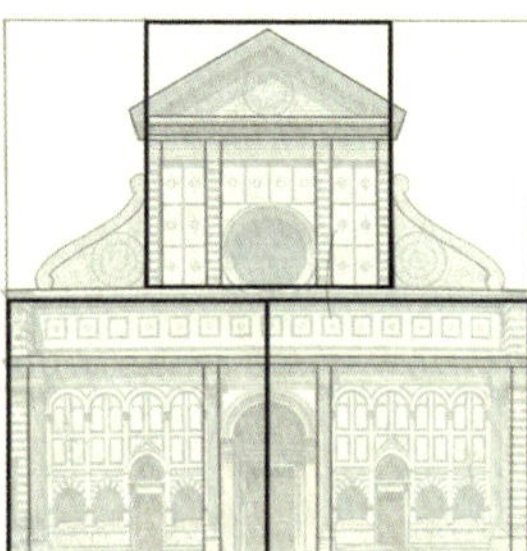

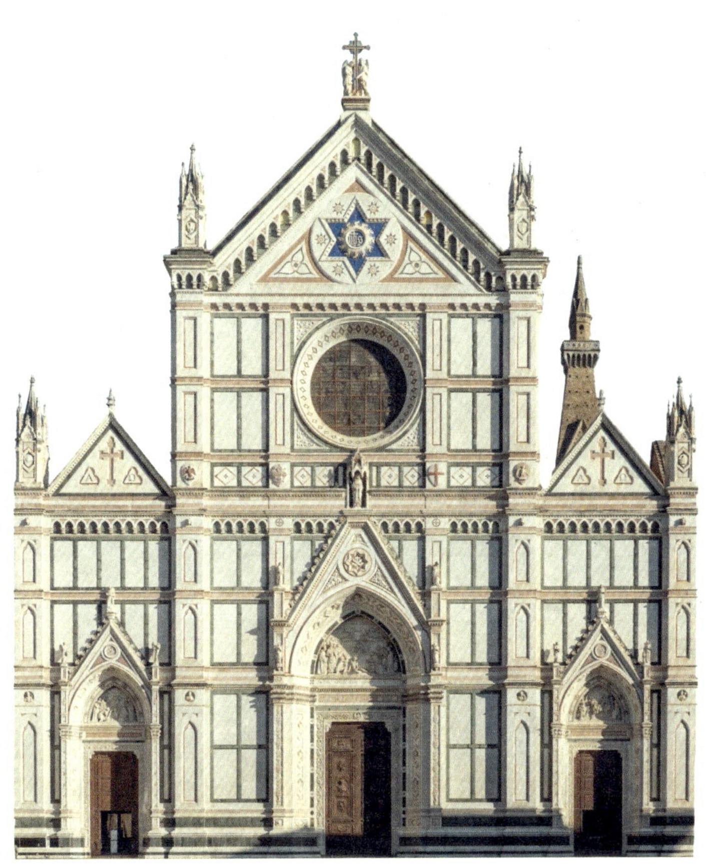

1. TAKE A STRAIGHT EDGE and find the squares directly on the picture of Santa Croce on a sheet of tracing paper over the image. Work from large shapes to small.

2. HAVE FUN finding as many squares and relationships as you can. Start by finding a similar breakdown of the facade as Santa Maria Novella shown on the opposite page. Then go in whatever direction you choose to explore the design.

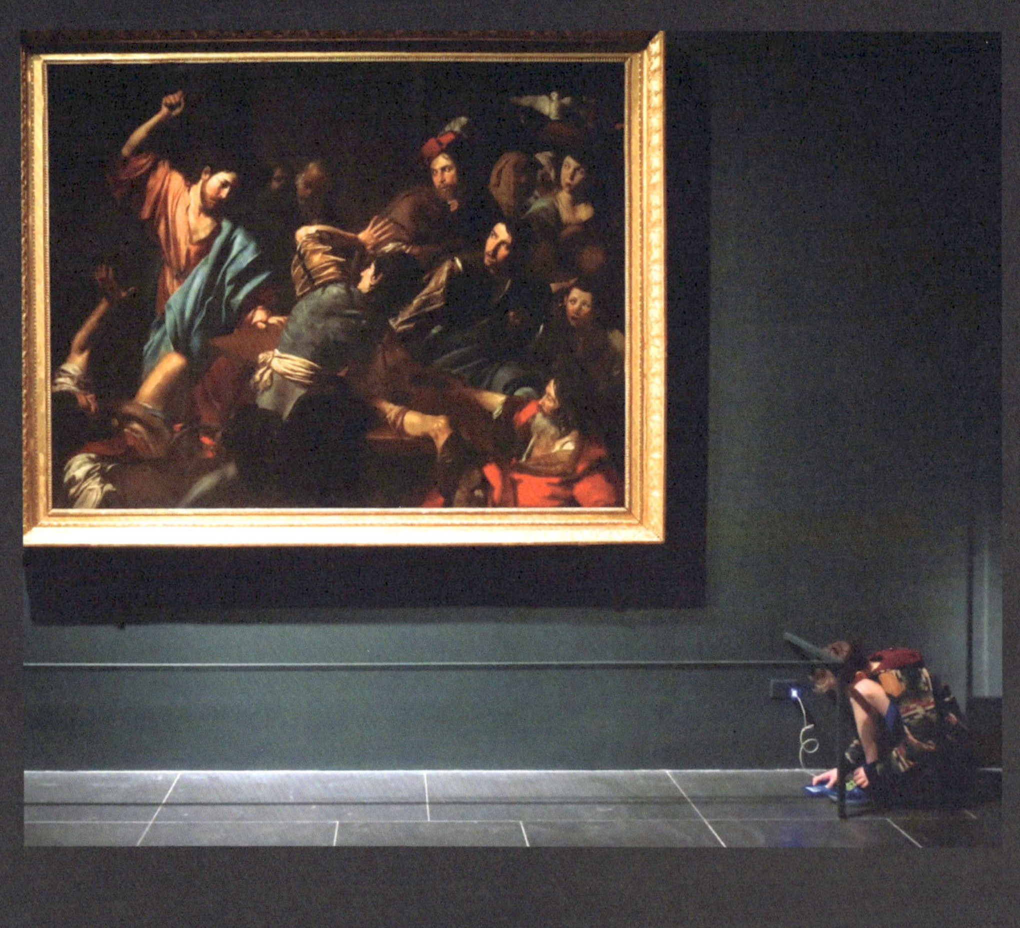

In less of the span of a single childhood,
Americans have merged
with their machines.

—JEFFREY CARR

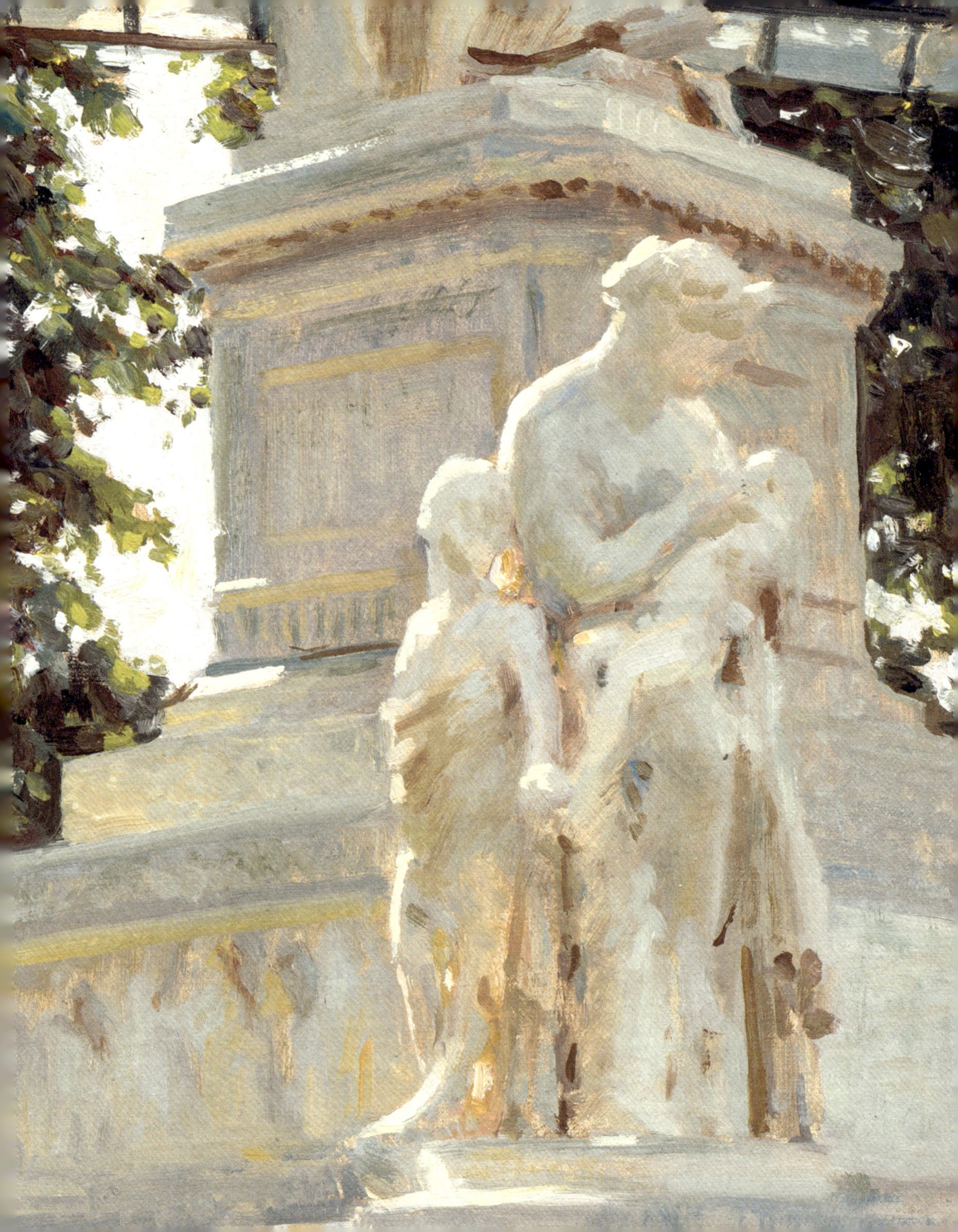

HOME OF THE MUSES

In art museums we feel less alone
in the face of what we ourselves see
each day appearing and disappearing.
—JOHN BERGER

ONCE, MUSEUMS FUNCTIONED AS SECULAR TEMPLES, the seat where muses bestow inspiration. The visitor ascends the temple stairs and separates from the world only to emerge again changed. Now, those who go to museums spend seconds looking at works of art. Is it possible that we do not quite know what to look for?

These spaces are still important for many people. If I'm lucky and the muses are willing, I go to museums the way other people go to church—to feed my soul. The word *inspire* originates from the Latin *spirare*, "to breathe." There are many days that are depleting, like one long continuous exhale. Being gifted with inspiration brings renewal of the spirit and energy, allowing us to inhale and be replenished. Art can be just such a breath.

My habit when exploring a museum is to stroll through the galleries to familiarize myself with the layout and collection, looking wherever interests me without pressure or expectations. Rather than try to see everything, I spend time with those pieces that most resonate with me without distraction or time limits. It's then that my spirit lifts.

I planned just such a day at the National Gallery of Scotland. I was on my initial survey mission, when I saw in one corner of an octagonal room against a scarlet gallery wall, a painting so small and dark it seemed barely there. The grand paintings on either side epitomize the wealth of nations, large and opulent. By contrast, this modest portrait peers through the gallery casting a depressive gloom, like a homely introvert in a corner at a party. Rembrandt, at age fifty-one, stares at us from across time out of a dark period of his life. This piece was painted a year after his 1657 bankruptcy, which required the auctioning off of both his house and art collection. It was a public humiliation and a record that his life hadn't gone to plan.

At first glance, the portrait appears to be one continuous tonal note of umber, like a gray Seattle sky slipping into nightfall. From the background to the shirt, collar, hat, and hair, there is only a breath of light to differentiate one from another. Then the slowest of transitions from the dark background to the fleshy forms of the face. The detail is concentrated on the wrinkles and furrows and the careful modeling of the worried lines in the artist's forehead. The eye on the right appears grim and defiant; the one on the left, exhausted. I searched for clues of how Rembrandt created such a perfect illusion of life, yet although I can point to all the artistic elements, the painting transcends that kind of language. It embodies him like another form of flesh and spirit.

When we stand face-to-face, we see ourselves reflected back and have the opportunity for belonging. In this vulnerable self-portrait, Rembrandt gave us permission to stare, and we see him as he saw himself. His eyes have tears, and yet the face is more beautiful than the lit symmetry of a younger man. Could Rembrandt have sensed that in the future what is fragile and human would be most treasured?

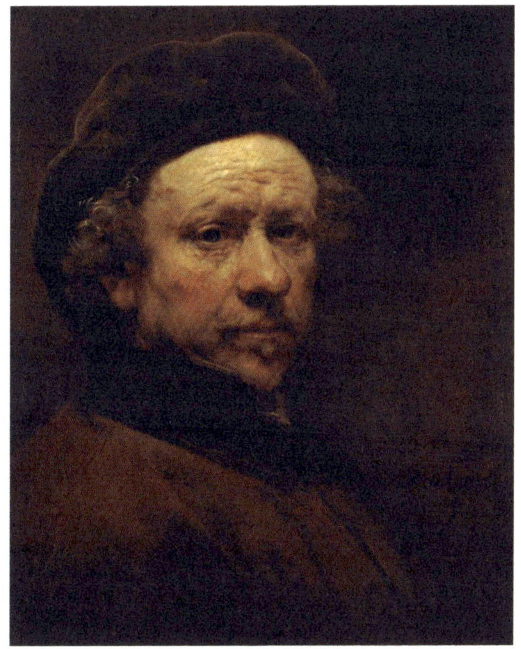

I spent most of my time that day in the National Gallery in front of this dark little painting, having a conversation of sorts with the artist. Just as I was getting ready to leave the room, I noticed a tall, beautiful young woman in shredded jeans striding directly up to Rembrandt's face. She didn't turn her head to look at Johannes Vermeer's *Christ in the House of Mary and Martha* on the left or the wall-size Anthony Van Dyck family portrait on the right; instead, she stood with her nose almost against Rembrandt's nose as if in a kiss. There was no personal space, no boundaries. It was so direct and intimate. I expected a guard to stop her, but no one did. And there she stayed, in his space with time collapsing, for longer than I thought possible.

ART
FOR CONSOLATION

One morning in March 2020, I left home for my studio expecting a hectic drive in one of the busiest commuter cities in the United States, yet the freeway was alarmingly empty. An eerie calm lay across Seattle. Unsettled, I canceled my plans for the workday and went instead to the Asian Art Museum.

Inside the museum, there is a room as black and empty as a cave except for three ancient stone Buddhas lit gently by a single beam of light from above. Gazing at each stone face, I wondered what trials the sculptors must have faced as they carved. What uncertainties of war, want, and illness made them afraid and made their efforts seem pointless? Time has long since filtered their stories out of living memory. Yet, the work survived to comfort me on a difficult day, a thousand years later.

Standing before those three Buddhas in the first week of the pandemic, I wept at the quiet assertion of these sculptures: that a lifetime spent making beautiful things contains something of enormous value—the enduring spirit of a human being.

When budgets are tight and times are hard, art is often the first thing to be jettisoned in the face of "real life." However, art gives hope, voice, and encouragement to the spirit. As much as life can hurt, art helps us make sense of our experiences. Art transforms our sorrow and darkness into meaning and beauty. Whether carved in stone or painted on canvas, this simple act of intimacy from artist to viewer is one of the most human experiences we share.

It's been over 45,000 years since the first hand drew a piece of ocher across a cave wall. Art predates civilization and is etched into our first consciousness. At its essence, great art is a form of electricity whose living current runs through us. It's a power, like love is a power.

Remember this the next time you go into the studio and wonder, "*What's the point?*" That this trial will pass, as they all do, and on that day your gifts will be needed to instill hope through your imagination. When the noise and news of the day fade into history, your art could be there waiting ready to meet someone on a hard day a millennia beyond our imagination.

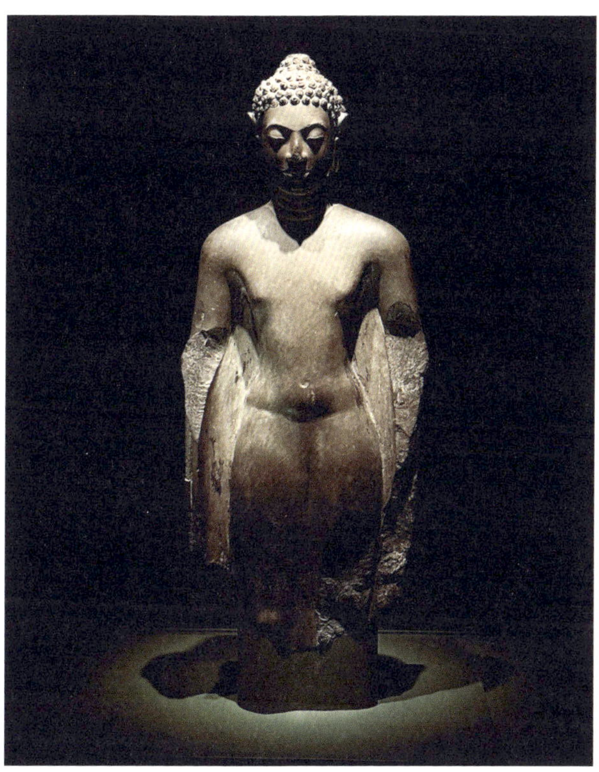

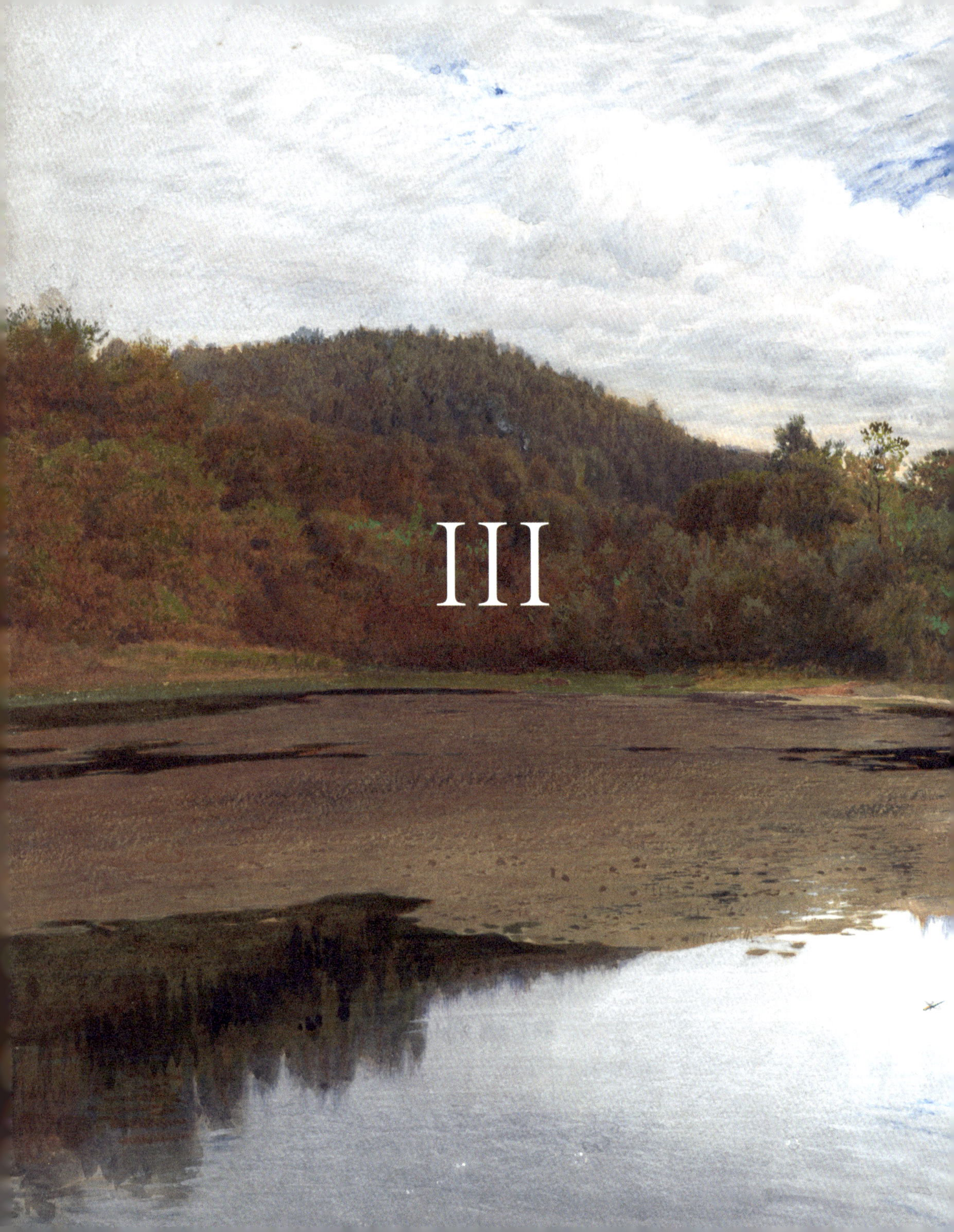

III

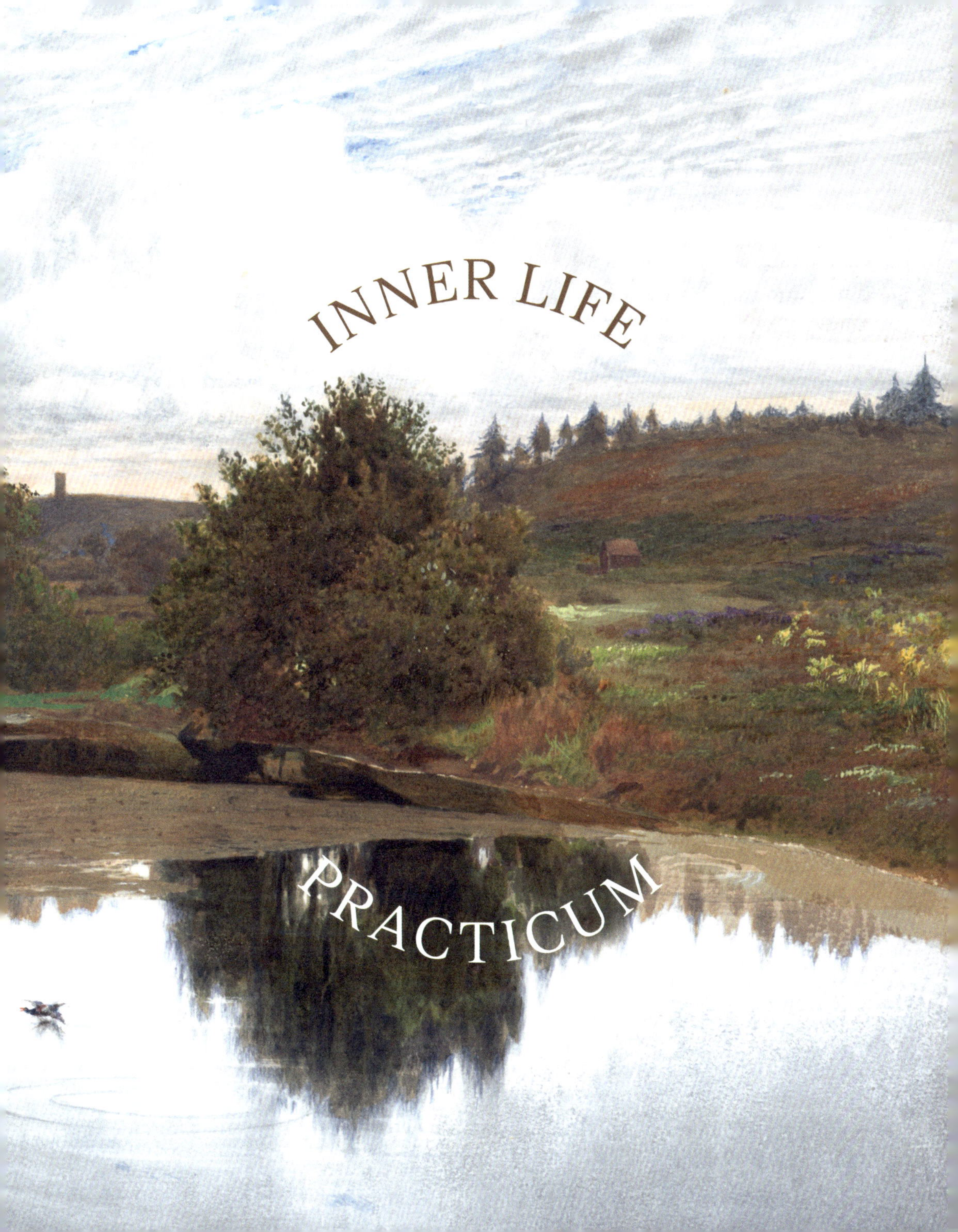
INNER LIFE
PRACTICUM

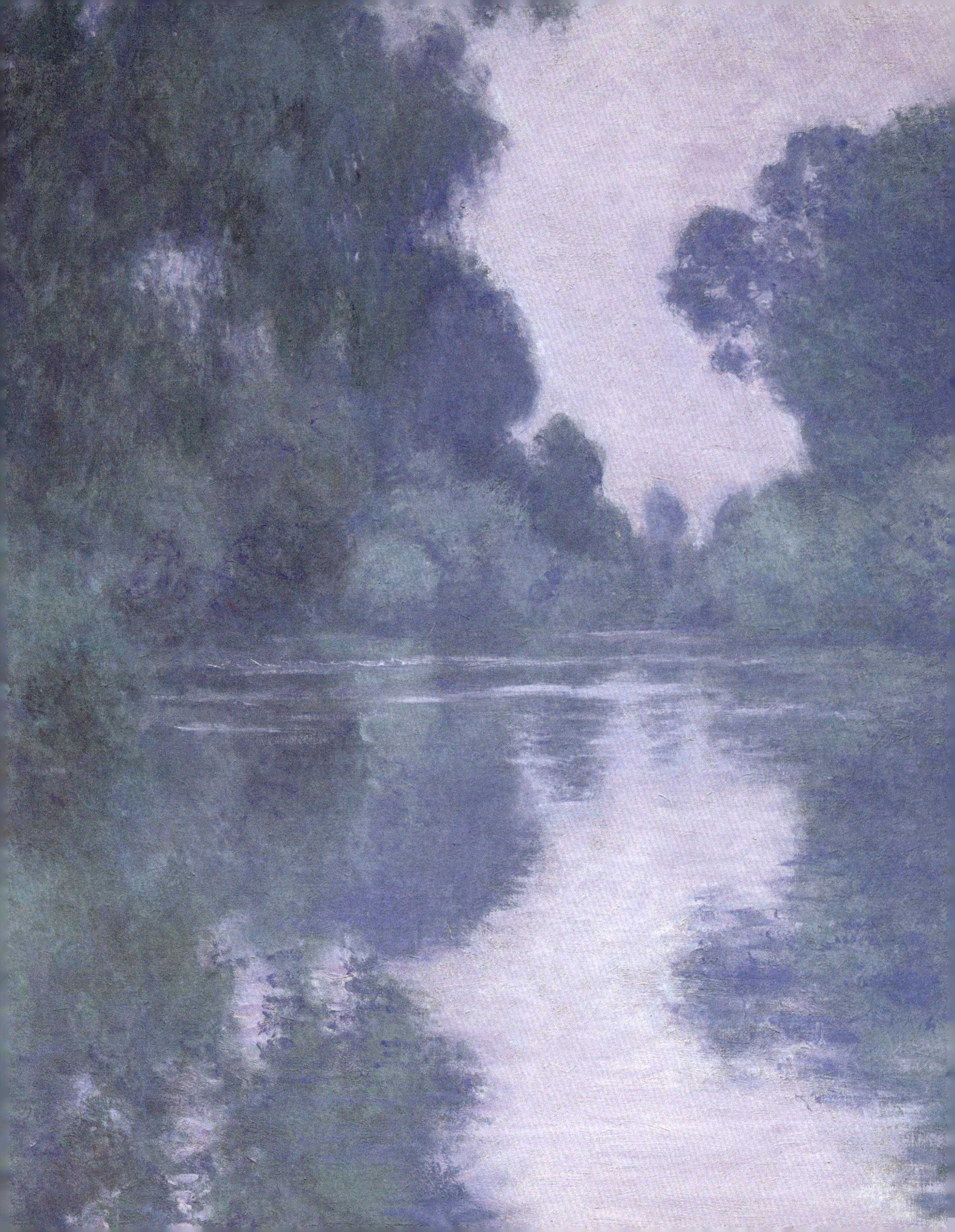

PAINTING WITH WORDS

DOCTOR, you say there are no haloes
around the streetlights in Paris
and what I see is an aberration
caused by old age, an affliction.
I tell you it has taken me all my life
to arrive at the vision of gas lamps as angels,
to soften and blur and finally banish
the edges you regret I don't see,
to learn that the line I called the horizon
does not exist and sky and water,
so long apart, are the same state of being.

—FROM "MONET REFUSES THE OPERATION" BY LISEL MUELLER

I TOOK A WEEKEND POETRY WORKSHOP, keeping a friend company with the vague notion of self-improvement. The result was me, sitting on a wild northwestern beach, spending hours searching for synonyms for the color gray: steel, flint, flannel, mica. My mind was pacing a room the size of a ring box. I didn't realize that poetry was so different from casual speech.

Original thought takes time. So, the slow gains of pulling ideas into consciousness are hard-won.

Who better to enlist than a poet to help sensitize our minds to the art of words? The callings of the poet and the painter overlap. One uses words on paper, the other paint on canvas, yet both spin inner thought into outer expression. Our words influence our thoughts as much as our thoughts influence our words. A shrinking vocabulary diminishes our capacity for critical thought while limited ideas need hardly more than an emoji for expression. Perhaps the painter can learn something about looking at art from these lovers of language.

The reading and writing of poetry can sensitize us to the power of words. It can also lead us into a deeper experience of art. An ekphrastic poem is an ancient art form centered on a vivid written encounter with visual art. It is the best possible type of feedback loop: The writer gives voice to the painting and through their eyes we are led into a deeper understanding of an original work.

Kurt Vonnegut, late in life, was sent a letter from some high school students who wanted him to visit their school. In a response letter that has gone viral, he wrote back that there was no need for a visit because what he had to say wouldn't take long. He earnestly encouraged them to practice art not for money or recognition but to enlarge themselves. He suggested they write a six-line poem about any subject and keep it to themselves. They were to make it as good as they could and then tear it up into tiny pieces and throw it away, showing it to no one. By doing this, he explained:

> You will find that you have already been
> gloriously rewarded for your poem.
> You have experienced becoming,
> learned a lot more about what's inside you,
> and you have made your soul grow.

BEGINNER'S GUIDE TO EKPHRASIS

POET AND EDUCATOR Christine Perrin, director of writing at Messiah College, has taught literature and creative writing at Johns Hopkins University with Gordon College's Orvieto Program. In this section she will guide you through making your own poem.

The twin arts of literature and painting spring from the same impulse; they echo and enlarge each other. The poet has many points of access from which to start a poem. If you see the original artwork, you can discuss its texture, its history, or its presence in space. Or you can have the work of art speak for itself directly in the first person.

When writing your poem, there is no single correct way to do this, and the goal remains to make an art object that that pleases others and gives others access to an encounter. The writer gets to decide how this comes together.

SOME CREATIVE WAYS POETS ENGAGE WITH VISUAL ART

- Talk to the painting
- Make the painting speak to the viewer
- Meditate upon your encounter with the artwork
- Question how the medium and scale contribute to the meaning of the artwork
- Reflect upon your own life, and see if the artwork ties into your own experience

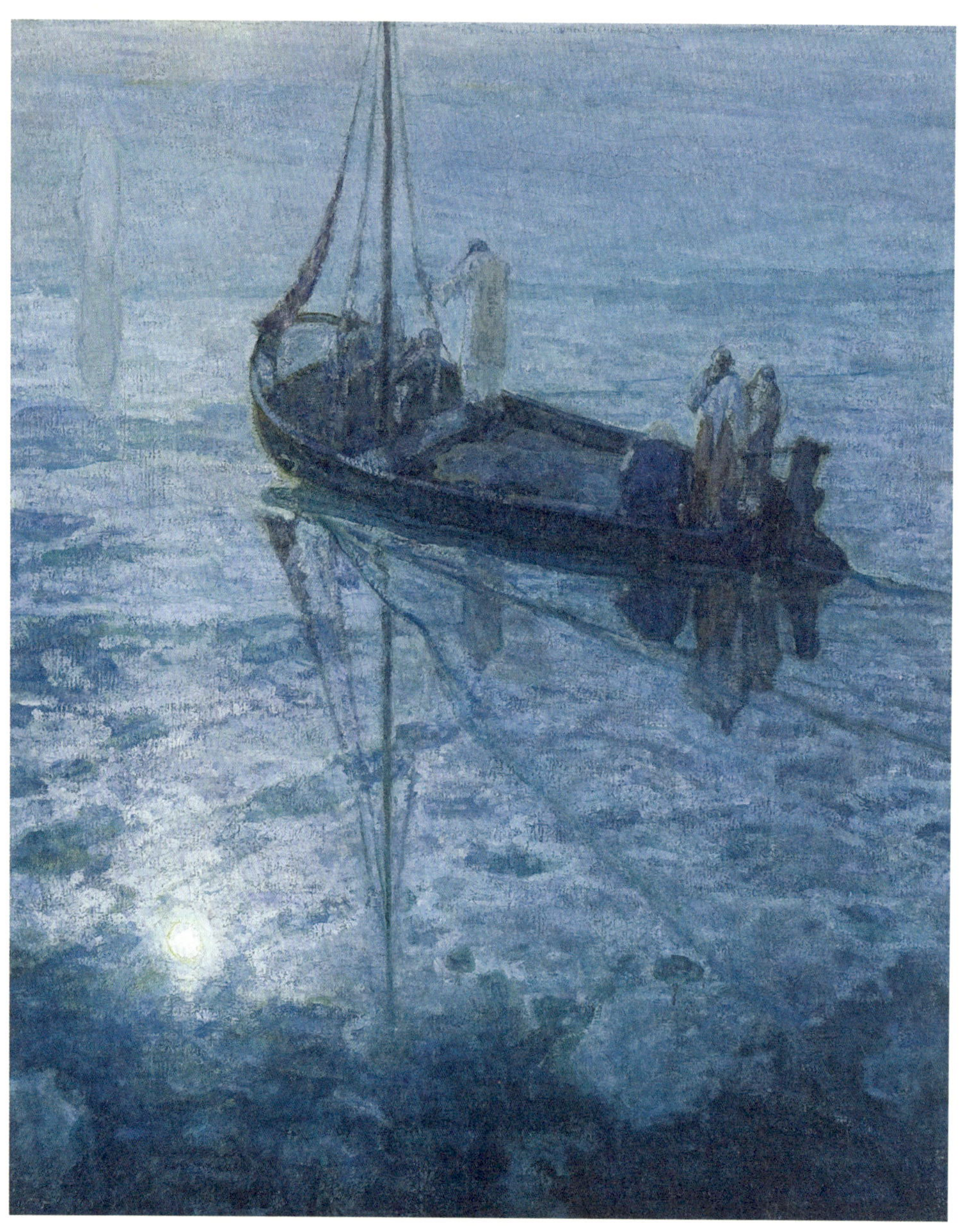

WRITE A POEM

POETRY ALLOWS US to look longer and deeper at art. Enjoy this process without worrying about making a beautiful poem. There is no right or wrong way to start.

1. SPEND a few minutes observing the painting on the opposite page or choose another work of art.

2. START writing for four minutes without lifting your pencil to edit or re-read. You can simply start with the words, "I see ______." What is your general impression? Does something catch your eye?

You can leave it as is and read your poem aloud. Or take it further.

3. REFINE what you've written by underlining what feels most resonant from your writing. Focus on visual or emotional points of interest.

4. UNDERLINE the line of your poem that you like the best, and on a fresh sheet of paper, use it as a template line to flesh out the rest of the poem.

5. TITLE the work–as to encircle the impression of the painting you have observed and the poem created. (Insert applause and a backslap here.)

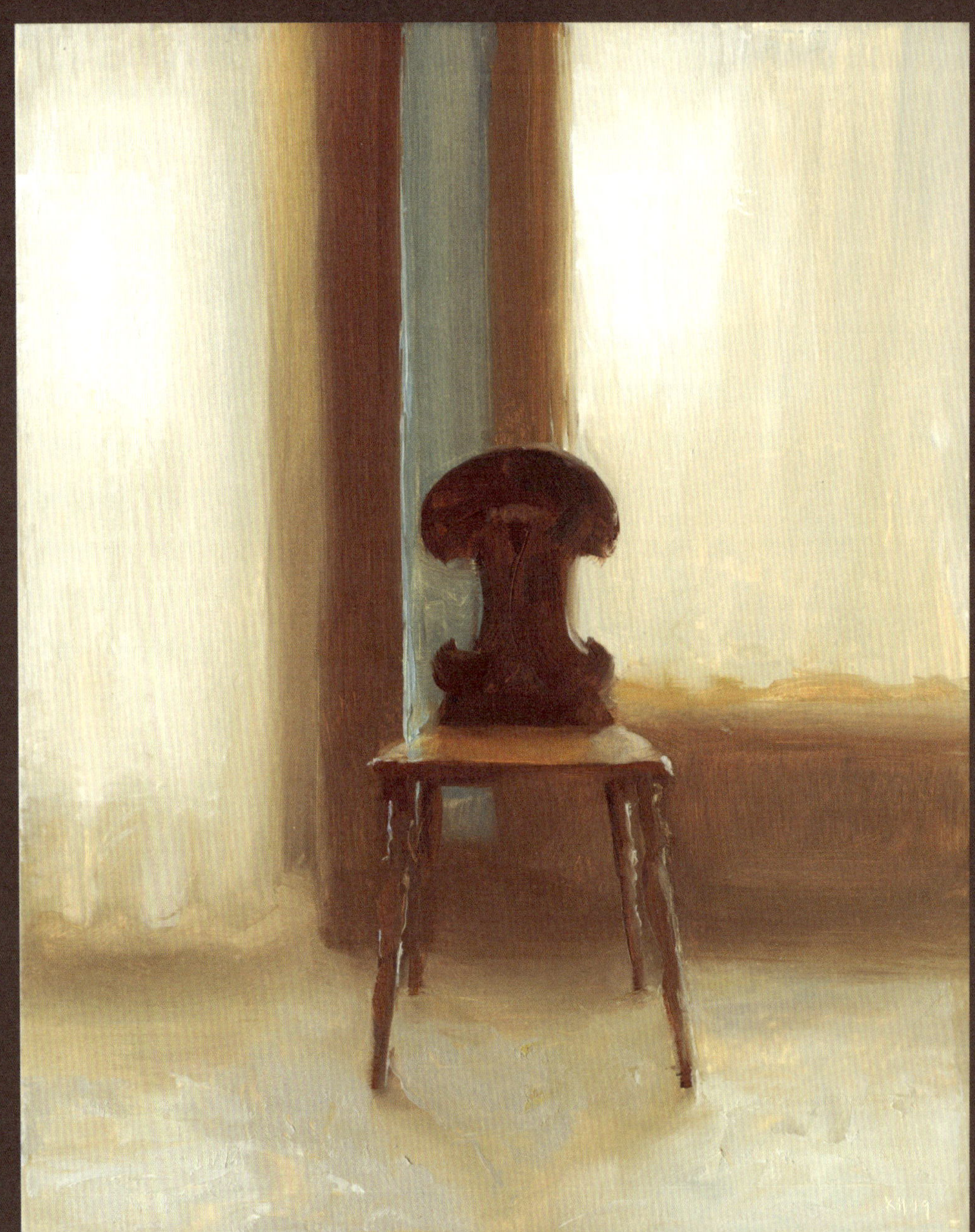

Sit in a room and read—
and read and read.
And read the right books
by the right people.
Your mind is brought
onto that level,
and you have a nice, mild,
slow-burning rapture
all the time.

—JOSEPH CAMPBELL

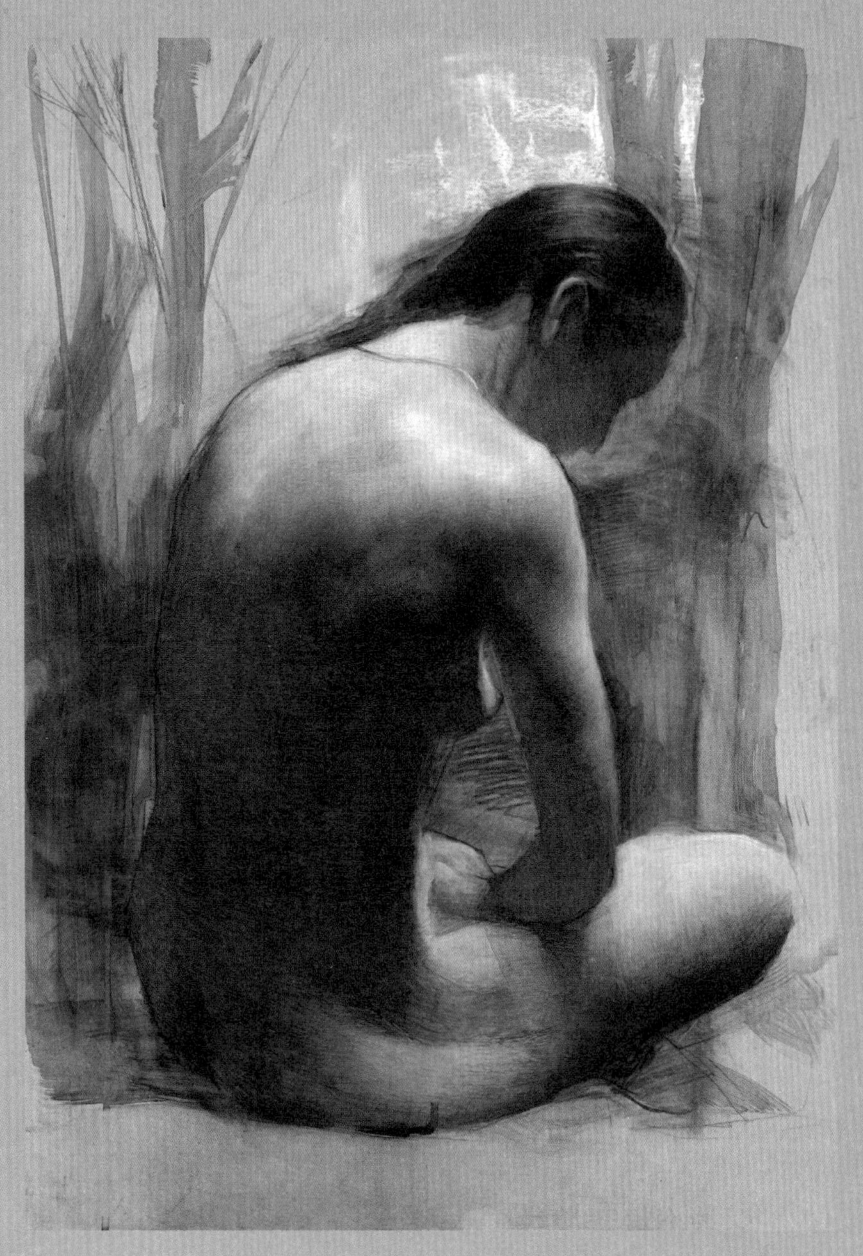

FIRE
IN BLACK AND WHITE

Reading is on the threshold
of a spiritual life . . .
—MARCEL PROUST

I'VE BEEN RESCUED MORE THAN ONCE by a book. Words and words and words . . . then suddenly a voice in my ear, a finger leveled at the center of my chest. The booming voice of a prophet or a whisper of friendship. In both, I am called forward.

Once, grieving a loss, I spent a night in a cottage in the woods for space to think. I randomly chose *Emerson's Essays* from a shelf of decorative books. I flipped to the center and started reading. Father Emerson preached to me that night: The aim of nature is growth not happiness. The unplayable losses of life are a divine expansion. The warning against looking back and the admonition to leave the tent of tears.

I shut the book, and I was different. I still am.

Artists can debate which subject matter is the highest form of art. Is social realism more important than floral painting, or was it the other way around? Yet the image isn't always the message nor is the narrative of a story. Sometimes it's the application of paint or the sound and beauty of words that can lead one to glory.

Many of us can point to a time when text came alive for us. My friend Will Berkovitz's father often read him his favorite poem, "The

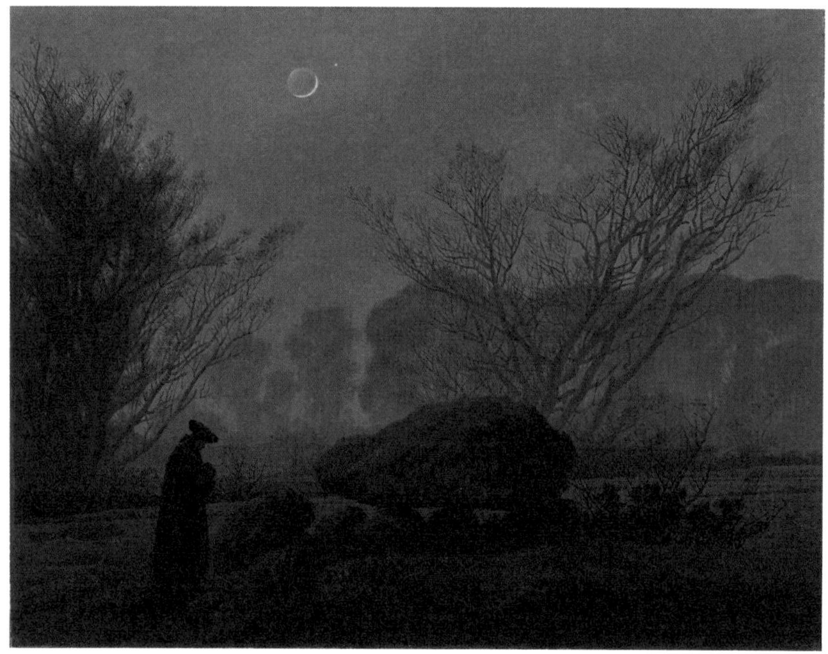

Highwayman" by Alfred Noyes. It starts, "The wind was a torrent of darkness among the gusty trees . . ." My mother also used to read this to me when I was growing up.

His father told him to pay attention to each word, and for the first time a complete picture appeared in Will's mind's eye like a movie. Even now when he reads the poem to his own children, he hears the words in his father's voice. They have a texture he can almost taste.

The power of a book is found in collaboration between the mind of the reader and the mind of the writer. The artist understands this. Painting needs the retina and curiosity of the viewer, just like the poem on the page needs the mind and life experience of the reader. Libraries contain multitudes: each book a soul, filled with stories, experience, and wisdom spanning centuries. The daily lives of authors are filled with the same drama and distractions of living as ours, yet the very best books are an attempt at permanence. Through reading we are recipients of the world's knowledge from the best minds. Along the way my opinion is tested and my experience expanded. Reading is the only training in writing I have ever known, so I can fairly say that through reading I learned to write.

The author, like the painter, has an encounter and shapes it with as much skill and vision as they are allotted. There are thousands of tiny choices, each decision changing and sculpting the language. The meaning of the words are embedded in language, like the materials of a painting are part of the message of a picture, so read carefully. Look at the words, question them, weigh them, discuss them—because through them, we embody worlds within ourselves.

Nicholas Carr has observed, that, in the quiet and calm of the reader's deep attention, the attentiveness becomes part of the meaning of the poem. The bond between book reader and writer is a symbiotic one.

Reading creates a lattice of associations and meanings that enrich us and lead to deep thinking. So how can we get more out of reading? The quickest way is to ask questions about the text. By simply asking ourselves "*why*?" we are brought down deeper and deeper with each question, into the heart of meaning. Good text is like a kaleidoscope, and every time you turn it over in your mind, you see something new.

"THE MONUMENT," SCULPTOR AND DECORATOR.
A Monthly Trade and Art Magazine.
~~119 West 41st Street,~~ 503 FIFTH AVE, COR. 42nd STREET.

TWO DOLLARS PER ANNUM. WILSON MACDONALD, Editor.

New York, Apr 8. 1895.

L. C. Handy

Dear Sir

Mr Brady is here with me and he directs me to write to you and request make out a list of the War views all that you can send that refer to the Seventh Reg of New York — Make ~~out~~ slides of them for the Steriopticon — he wants about one hundred of the most interesting ones of groups and battle scenes that would be of interest — Brady is about to receive a Grand testimonial benefit here at the hands of his life long friends — He will of course pay you as soon as the benefit is over and

HANDWRITING

HANDWRITING HAS CHANGED through the ages to conform to the times. Here is a quick progression of cursive in the recent past. Irregularities make each hand's writing unique; it doesn't have the perfection of the font, but what we lose in precision we gain in personality. When I see an envelope with my mother's writing, it brings her presence to life in a way that an email in Times New Roman can't. Handwriting is the last vestige of drawing training available to many, sensitizing our eye for symmetry, proportion, and hand-eye dexterity. The push for efficiency and perfection has driven slower skills to the farthest margins.

Calligrapher Marie Hornback leads us through a brief tour of cursive:

COPPERPLATE

Copperplate

USED WIDELY in England and Europe for engraving text into copper plates for letterheads, invitations, announcements, etc. It was written solely by hand with pressure placed on the pen nib for every downstroke. It is a disciplined script that is made slowly.

SPENCERIAN

INFLUENCED by the shapes he saw in nature, Platt Rogers Spencer developed this American script. The pen is able to continue writing without lifting the point from the paper, called a running hand. There is little pressure used when writing the lowercase letters. The capitals, however, were embellished with shaded strokes created by pressure of the flexible nib of the pen.

ZANER-BLOSER

A SCRIPT OR CURSIVE handwriting system taught in some public schools today. It is monoline with no shaded strokes. It can be written with a pen or a pencil—or any other monoline writing instrument. Notice the much shorter ascender and descender loops. The loops are equal to the body height of the letters. It is efficient, but not as graceful as the other two scripts. It allows for quicker handwriting.

THE FONT

THE KEYBOARD has replaced handwriting for most of us. The clarity and speed of the digits of our fingers in a downward motion clicking a perfectly featureless version of ourselves. Writing and drawing both use a pencil with a dexterous hand.

DIRECTIONS

COPY the sentence.

Expressions of the heart,
not perfection, is the goal
of writing by hand.

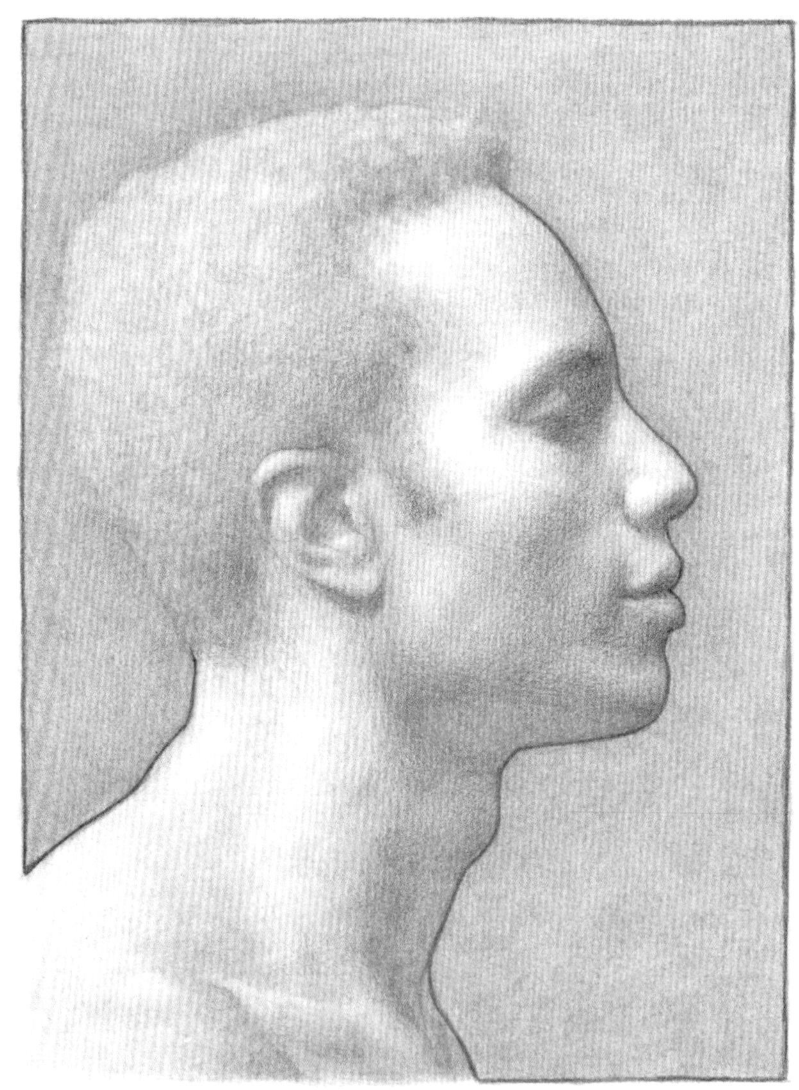

SEEING WITH OUR EARS

WE SEE NOT JUST WITH OUR EYES, but with all our senses. Emotional connections are often made without words. A hand held communicates love just as a smile makes us feel welcome. A tone of voice, a slump of shoulders, and the invisible weight we sense beyond words speak when someone says they are fine and yet we know they are not. Body language is universal. And when we are alert and open, there are many ways to see.

The American icon Ernest Hemingway believed that the best training for a writer is listening. He said, "Listen now. When people talk, listen completely. Don't be thinking about what you're going to say. Most people never listen. Nor do they observe." He also recommended you memorize what you see and feel when you walk into a room. (Try it, why not?) To be an artist we must be as close an observer as a writer.

Taking Hemmingway's words to heart, I dropped into a class for a few quick tips on compassionate listening. I should have known better.

I was paired with a stranger, a woman. Standing eye to eye I followed the directive to empty myself of thought and radiate as much love and empathy while not saying a word. I stared into my partner's eyes unguarded for ninety long seconds while violating every social norm in the process. Yet in that minute and a half, she moved from the back ground of my attention to the foreground.

It struck me that I have worked with people for years who have never felt as real to me as this person I looked at for ninety seconds but never spoke to. Real listening is a form of presence taking place in the eyes, heart, and mind and not only the ears. From that point on I integrated a listening component in my atelier.

When we truly see someone, it's a form of generosity, indistinguishable from love. Many of these signals are nonverbal allocations of attention, much like our painting practice. Deep connection with others is key to human happiness and among our most profound life experiences. Artists seek to create encounters just as sacred between viewers and our art.

I wondered, *if listening is so fundamental to human connection, why isn't it instinctive or at least easier?* To find out I asked Susan Partnow, senior facilitator for the Compassionate Listening Project, to meet me for a coffee.

Susan explained that to be a good listener we must be open—easy to say but difficult to do.

We are born openhearted and feel all our emotions. Yet being so open leaves us vulnerable to being hurt. There are times we are unwelcome, feel judged, and experience shame. We can develop defenses to protect ourselves. If defenses are the bricks walling in our heart, the mortar are the stories we tell ourselves, and then rehearse until they fix in place as truth. These protective measures help us avoid vulnerability, but they also keep us from connecting.

Yet when we are listened to without an agenda, we can experience a profound sense of belonging. Clara Moisello, PhD codirector of the New York Center for Nonviolent Communication, notes that in a caring space, when we are welcomed with acceptance and empathy, it's healing. The work of listening is to create that space.

To listen well—just like learning to see well—is a journey of a lifetime. Having friendships is a strong predictors of longevity and happiness. Close connection with other human beings gives us a sense of deep belonging and can be transformative. The times I have experienced this are rare, unforgettable, and feel like love.

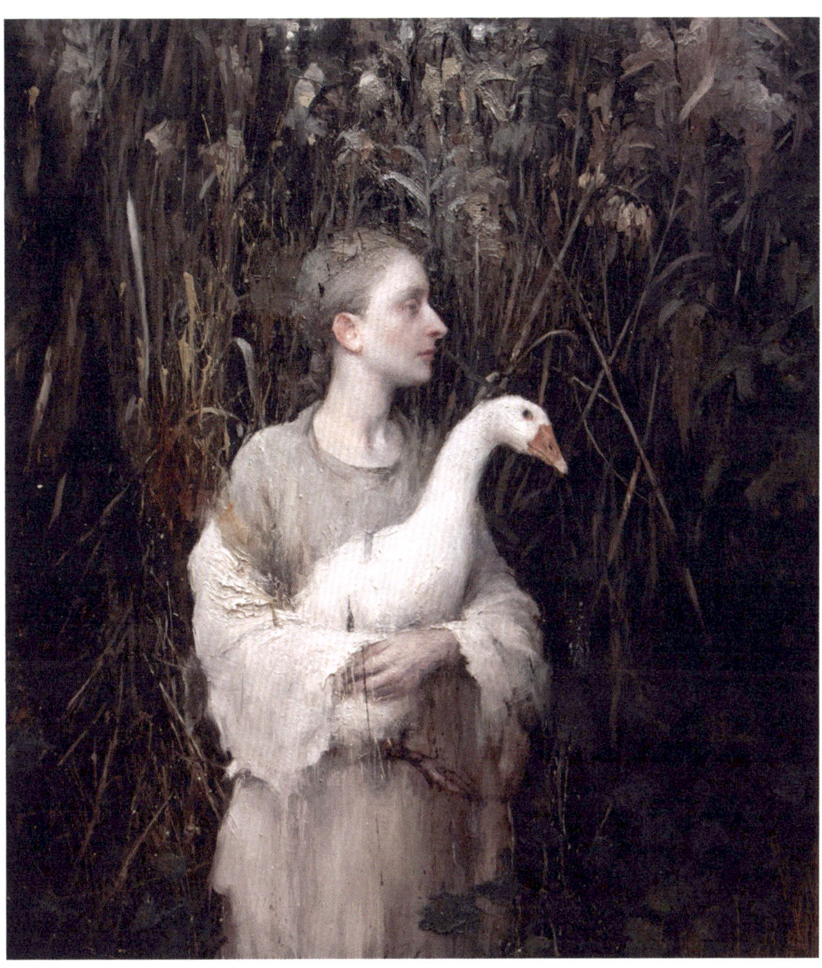

COMPASSIONATE LISTENING

THE FIRST STEP prepares us for an authentic encounter. The second step allows us to try deep listening for ourselves.

CENTERING

Take a moment to settle into your chair. Feel the earth beneath your feet. Feel the chair supporting you. Turn your attention to your breath.

As you inhale through your nose, notice the coolness of the air. As you exhale, notice the warmth. Allow your breath to expand your belly and feel it bring oxygen to every cell of your body. Breathe in empathy and patience and breathe out tension. Continue to pay attention to your breath for a few moments. Notice how your whole body feels more centered and calm. When you are ready, open your eyes.

LISTENING

In this exercise we practice completely listening to another person with empathy. The gift of listening is a form of hospitality.

1. FIND A PARTNER and sit opposite each other. One of you will be Partner 1, and the other will be Partner 2.
2. TO START, set a timer for three minutes.
3. EACH PERSON will take a turn talking: Partner 1 will go first and has three minutes to speak without interruption.
4. PARTNER 2 acts as the listener. The listener's job is to do nothing but be a silent, empathetic witness without giving advice or judging.
5. WHEN the first speaker is finished, the listener will show simple appreciation for the speaker, and quickly move on.
6. NOW switch roles. Partner 2 has a chance to share for three minutes while Partner 1 acts as the listener.

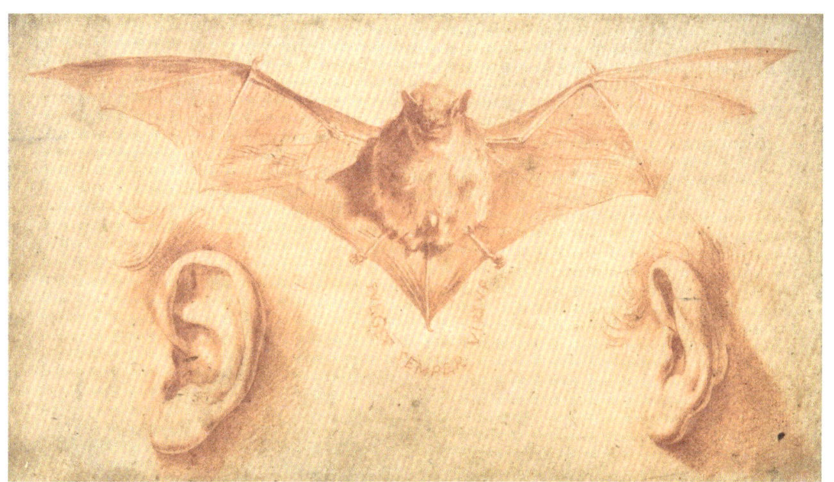

CONVERSATION STARTERS

WHAT do you think about before you go to sleep at night?

WHAT is the first thing you think about when you wake up in the morning?

WHAT would you like to experience more deeply in your life?

WOULD you prefer to be able to visit the past or to visit the future?

WHEN EACH PARTNER has acted as both speaker and listener, do you notice anything new?

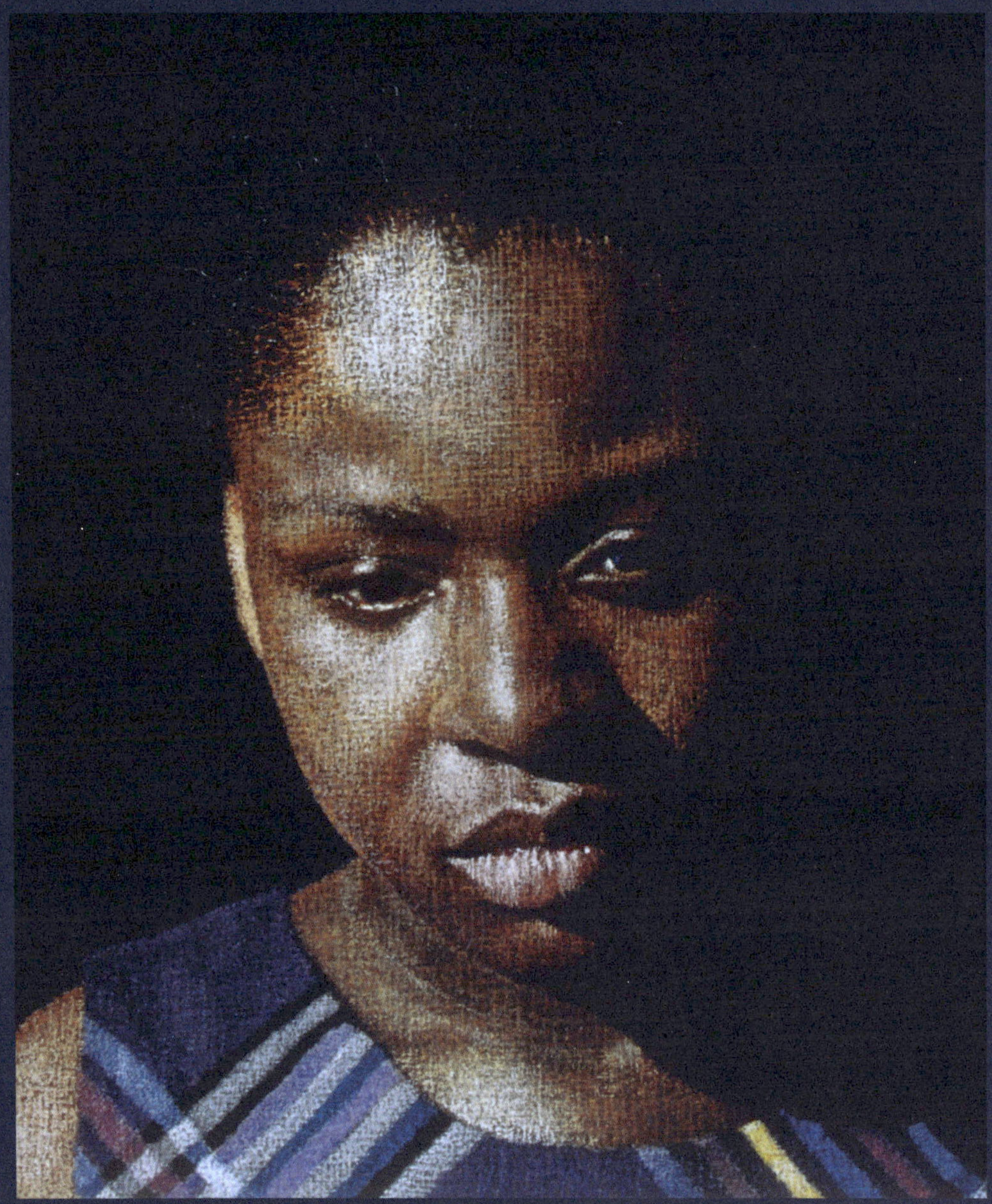

Out of this turning-within,
out of this immersion
in your own world,
poems come,
then you will not think of asking anyone
whether they are good or not.

—RAINER MARIA RILKE

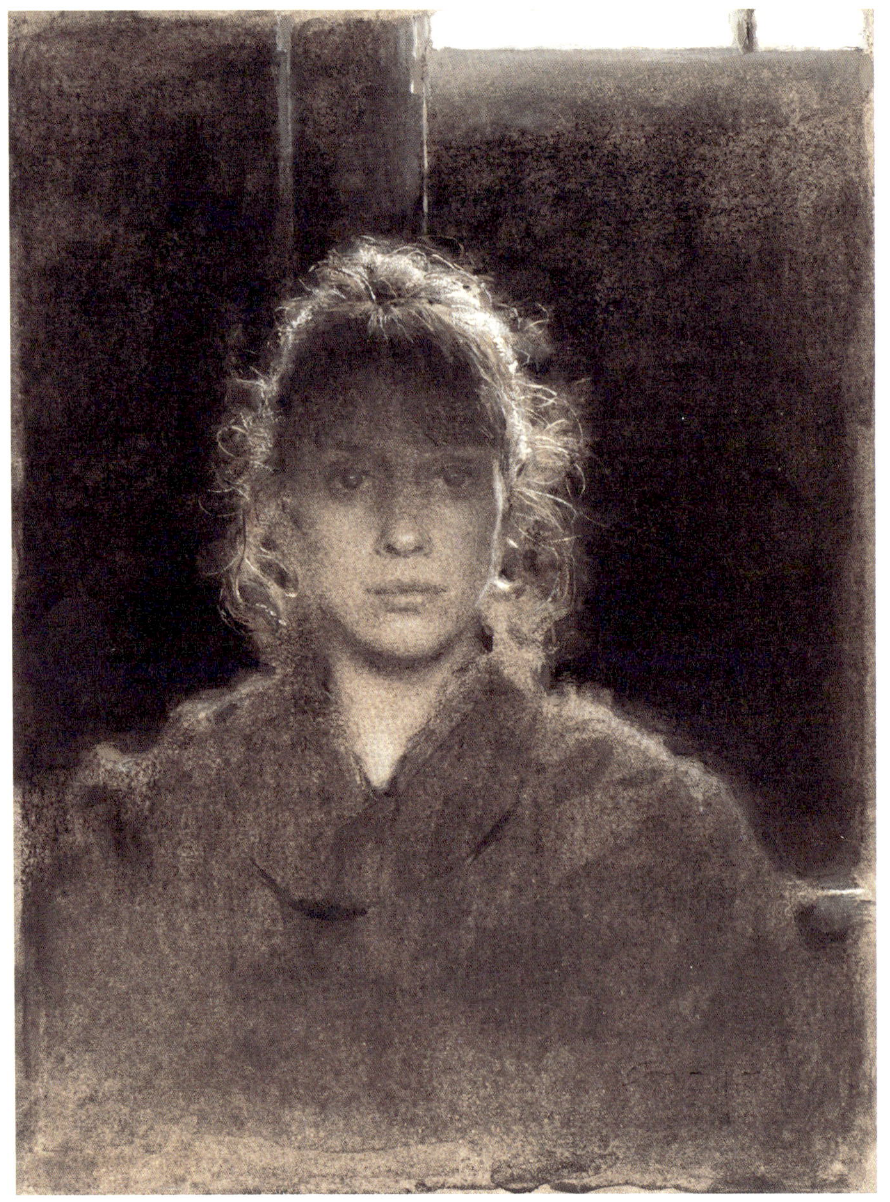

EPILOGUE

If men had postponed the search
for knowledge and beauty
until they were secure
the search would never have begun.

—C. S. LEWIS

ANTHEM

ARTISTS ARE generally not the most practical of God's creatures nor the first listed on people's emergency contact list—for a variety of reasons. We may not notice that the car is out of oil or that money must be saved for retirement. We are unaware that no one cleaned the bathroom (or any other room). We also scrupulously avoid official-sounding letters. And yet the artist may be obsessively concerned with the exact tilt of the portrait's upper lip or a seamless transition of pink to violet paint across a sky.

And for this reason, among others, we may appear unpromising early on. I remember Ms. Martin's third grade class when she cleaned my glasses and told me, "It's okay," after the fourth and last egg for our Pennsylvania Dutch egg decorating class rolled off my desk and broke on the floor. Or the elementary school guidance counselor who said, "You will never become an artist, because you can't even spell it."

Things like this happen to artists when they are young, and perhaps it singles us out in some way. Gustave Flaubert was chastised for licking the green stuff off pennies. He was going to be brilliant, but, in the meantime, he was a mess.

Flaubert wrote to his mom 1850:

> When I ask myself:
> What shall I write? What will I be good for?
> Where shall I live? What path shall I follow?
> I am full of doubts and indecisions.
> At every stage of my life I have shirked,
> in just this way, facing my problems, and
> shall die at sixty before having formed any opinion
> concerning myself, or perhaps,
> written anything
> that would have shown me my capabilities.

Many artists follow their own timeline, and their interests can be wonderfully out of sync with the larger world. When I drove my friend for radiation treatment, we discussed our dreams. He dreamed of arriving at a painting class without a canvas or paints and leaving embarrassed. Here is a man being treated for cancer and yet was anxious about painting.

But make no mistake: regardless of how well or poorly the artist performs the tasks of daily living, they have an important role. The artist holds the world's imagination. Art isn't an invention of civilization; it's an expression of our humanness.

Let's establish a new metric for status based on our capacity for self-growth and wonder.

Similarly, my uncle, a doctor, took up art. Tired of illness, he longed to be pulled more deeply into living. He was seeking what was missing from his world at large. Art can save a life, and in many cases, the artist themselves is saved first.

The hearts of the painter and poet are large enough to hold both the news of the day alongside the concerns of the soul. More than that, it is essential that we hold both. Artists of old understood this. Take Sanford Robinson Gifford, for example: A golden light reflects off the water in his paintings, with air so still that even the wind holds its breath. Yet some of his landscapes were painted while The Civil War raged. Beauty, meaning, and purpose are as fundamental to the human orbit as gravity.

In the early days of the Russian invasion of Ukraine, I saw a video of a young woman playing the violin for a dozen people hiding from bombs in her family's basement. Her optimism and music were a symbol of resilience and hope. For all I know, she showed up late to every class and without her pencil. And yet her playing a long slow note on her violin in a time of desperate fear makes her a legend.

Artist, your path to mastery is not a straight one, and it can't be rushed. It is exactly the length and duration it needs to be. You are following a sound only you can hear to wherever it may lead. Through you we learn that there's more to life than we can see with our eyes, that there are things that cannot be bought but only experienced. And through you we experience a reenchantment of the world.

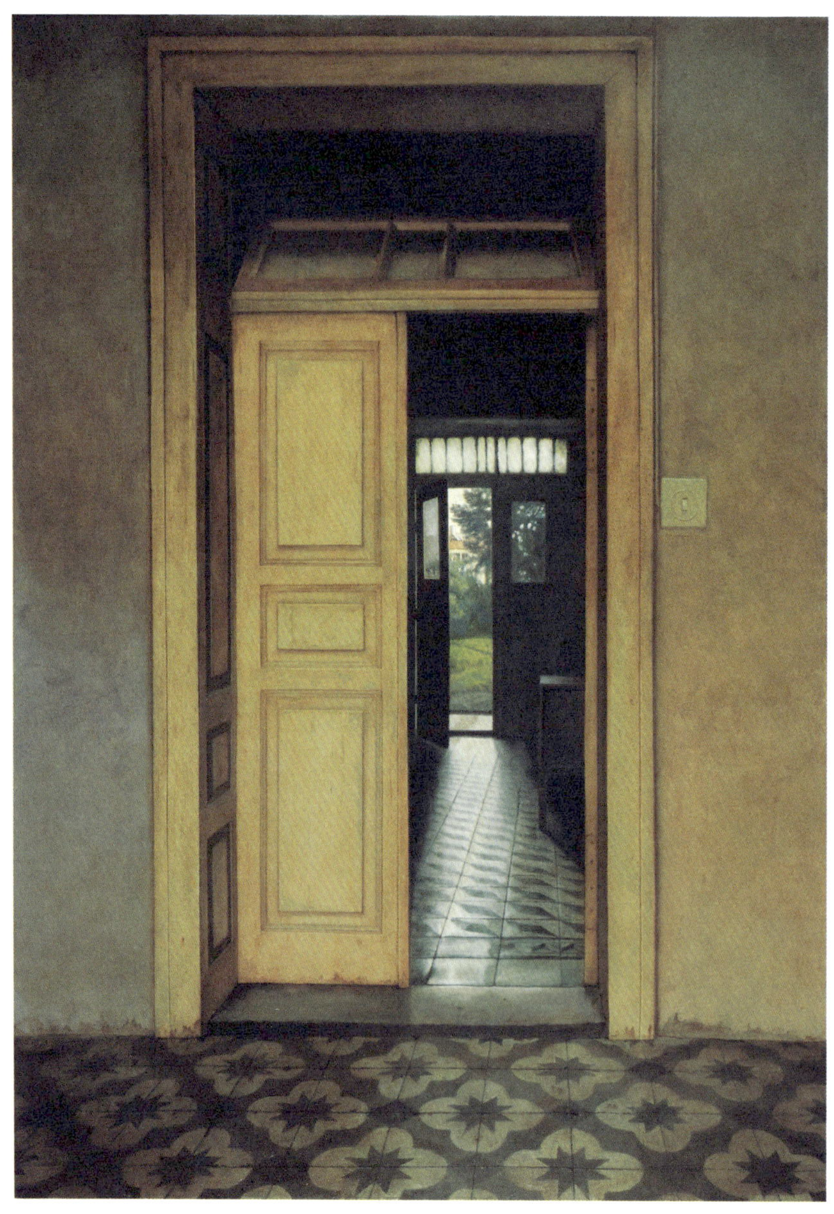

ACKNOWLEDGMENTS

WHO ARE WE WITHOUT OUR FRIENDS? This book would never have been created without the support of Laura Burt, whose editorial guidance and friendship was invaluable from the start. I am deeply grateful to Senior Editor at Monacelli Press, Carla Sakamoto, whose belief in this project shaped each page. Jessica Fleischmann, Creative Director of Still Room, who beautifully designed this book. Michael Vagnetti, Production Director, for your outstanding work. Many thanks to the contributors for many wonderful conversations: Christine Perrin, Susan Partnow, Clara Moisello, Will Berkovitz, Mark Kang-O'Higgins, Marie Hornback, Dr. Jason Barton, and Deborah Paris. Jun Danenhower, for help in researching caption information. And artist Amaya Gurpide, whose tenacity helped secure the inclusion of important images. My deep appreciation to all the artists who shared their work in this book. The beauty, skill, and imagination in your art leaves the world better than you found it. Much love to my remarkable family who bring so much mirth and meaning to my life.

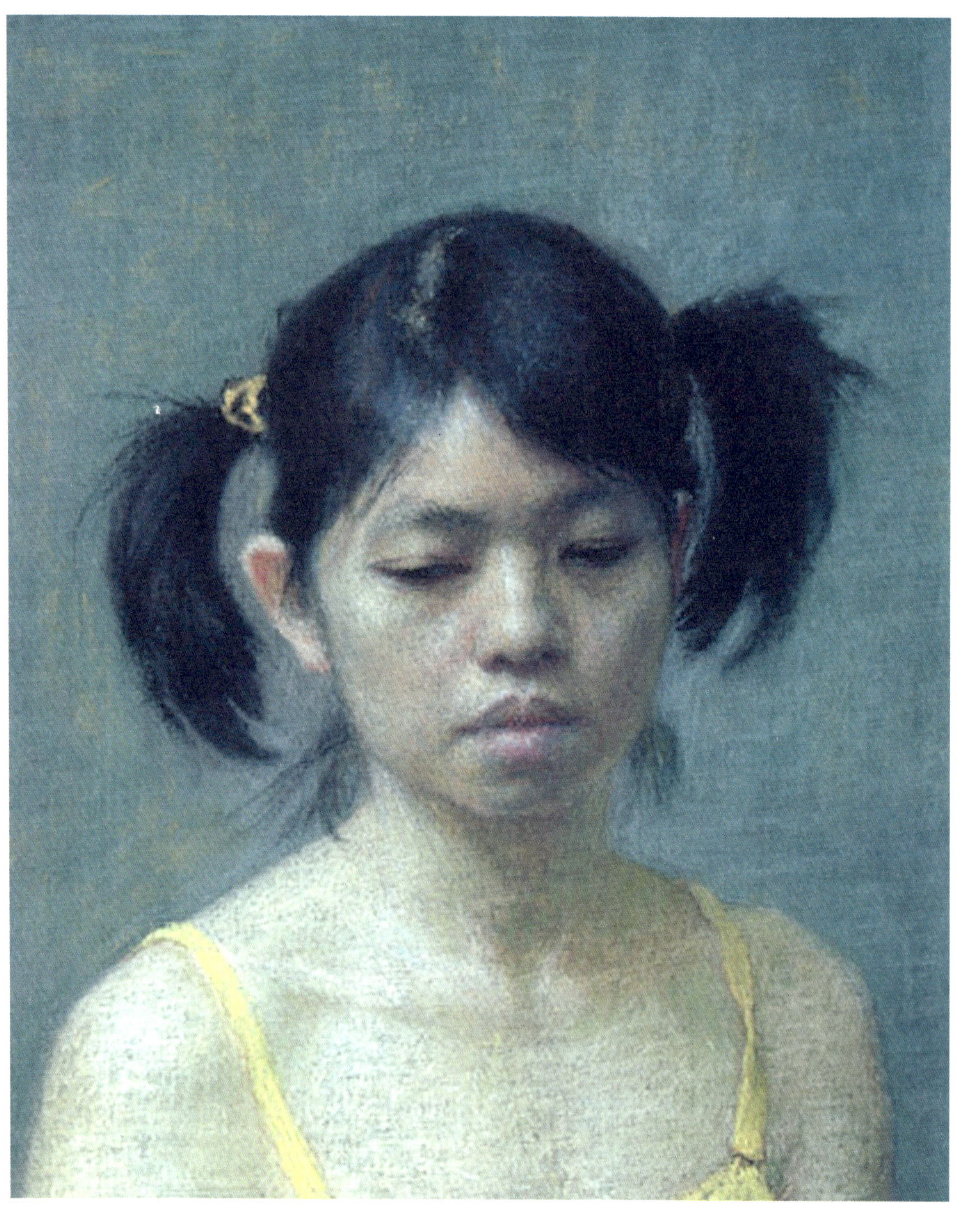

BIBLIOGRAPHY

Baudelaire, Charles. *Salon of 1846.* New York: David Zwirner Books, 2021.

Berger, John. *The Shape of a Pocket.* New York: Pantheon Books, 2002.

Campbell, Joseph, and Bill Moyers. *The Power of Myth.* New York: Bantam Doubleday Dell Publishing Group, 1991.

Carr, Nicholas G. *The Shallows: What the Internet Is Doing to Our Brains.* New York: W.W. Norton, 2011.

Emerson, Ralph Waldo. *The Works of Ralph Waldo Emerson*, Vol. 6: The Conduct of Life. Boston and New York: Fireside Edition, 1909.

Klinkenborg, Verlyn. *Several Short Sentences about Writing.* New York: Alfred A. Knopf, 2012.

MacDonald, George. *The Princess and the Goblin.* New York: Macmillan, 1951.

Mueller, Lisel. "Monet Refuses the Operation." In *Second Language.* Baton Rouge: Louisiana State University Press, 1986.

O'Donoghue, John. "On the Inner Landscape of Beauty" interview on the *On Being* podcast with Krista Tippett. September 23, 2019.

Perec, Georges. "Brief Notes on the Art and Manner of Arranging One's Books." In *Species of Spaces and Other Pieces*. London: Penguin, 1999.

Reznikoff, Charles. "Jerusalem the Golden: 66." In *The Poems of Charles Reznikoff: 1918–1975*, ed. Seamus Cooney. Boston: Black Sparrow/David R. Godine, 2005.

Rilke, Rainer Maria. *Letters to a Young Poet*. Penguin Little Black Classics. London: Penguin Classics. 2016.

Smith, Patti. *Devotion (Why I Write).* New Haven, CT: Yale University Press, 2017.

Sullivan, Louis H. *A System of Architectural Ornament*. New York: Rizzoli, 1990.

Thoreau, Henry David. *Journal of Henry D. Thoreau.* 14 vols. Boston: Houghton Mifflin, 1949.

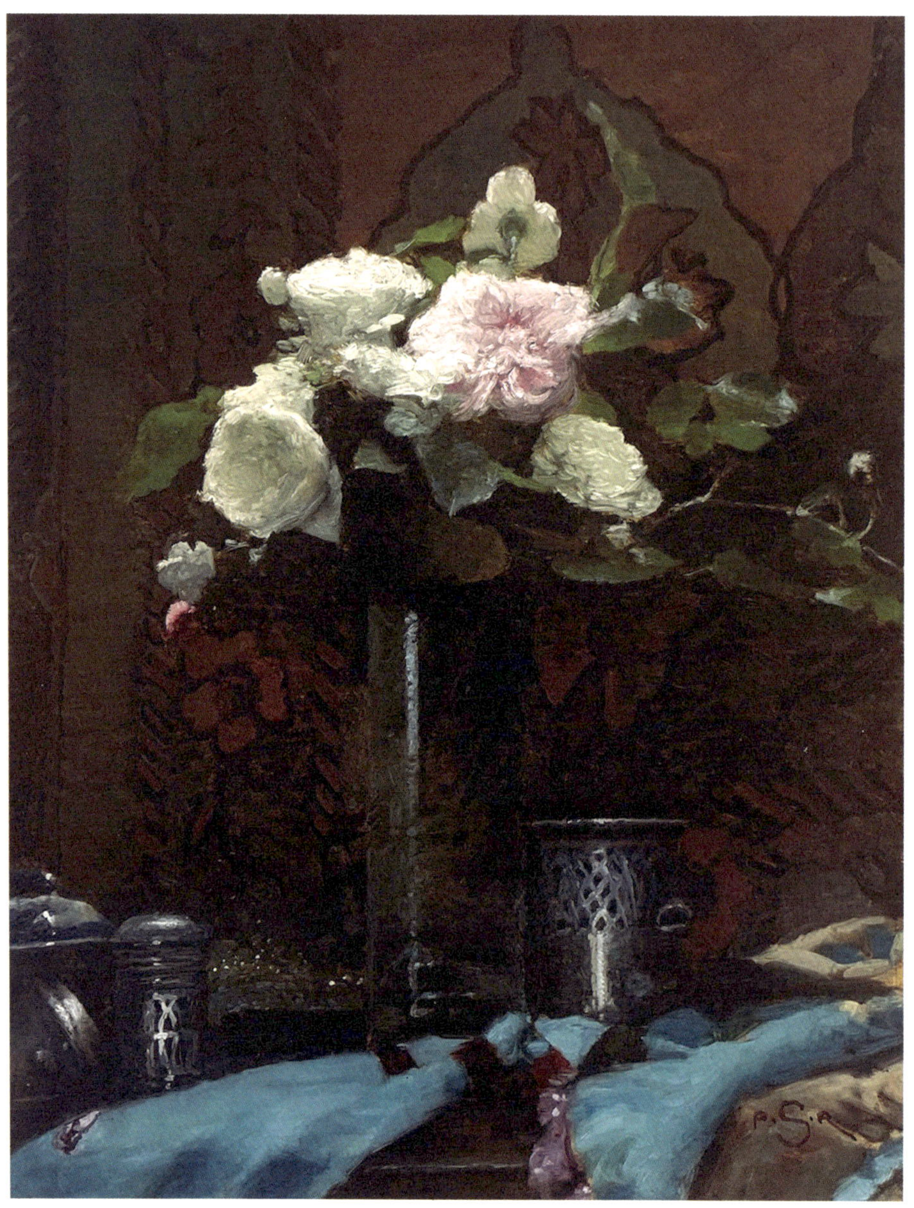

ARTWORK CREDITS

COVER IMAGE
Anonymous
Lover's Eyes (locket), 1840
Watercolor on ivory; 1 × ¾ in.
(2.5 × 1.9 cm)
Metropolitan Museum of Art
(This image was made as a locket
to be worn by an admirer)

OPENING ENDPAPER
John Frederick Kensett
Lake George, 1869
Oil on canvas; 44⅛ × 66⅜ in.
(112.1 × 168.6 cm)
Metropolitan Museum of Fine Art;
Bequest of Maria DeWitt Jesup,
from the collection of her husband,
Morris K. Jesup

HALF-TITLE PAGE
John Frederick Kensett
Newport Rocks, 1872
Oil on canvas; 31 × 48 in. (78.7 × 121.9 cm)
Metropolitan Museum of Art;
Gift of Thomas Kensett

TITLE PAGE
Abbott Handerson Thayer
Study of a Young Woman,
c. 1895
Pencil on paperboard;
13¼ × 10¼ in. (33.7 × 26 cm)
Smithsonian American Art Museum;
Gift of John Gellatly

DEDICATION PAGE
Leon Dabo
Evening on the Hudson (detail), 1907-8
Oil on canvas; 27⅛ × 36⅛ in.
(68.9 × 91.7 cm)
Smithsonian American Art Museum;
Gift of William T. Evans

PAGES 6-7
John Constable
Cloud Study, 1821
Oil on paper laid on panel;
8⅜ × 11½ in. (21.3 × 29.2 cm)
Yale Center for British Art, New Haven,
Paul Mellon Collection

PAGE 8
Julio Reyes
Heart of August, 2018
Egg tempera on panel; 10 × 9 in.
(25.4 × 22.9 cm)
Private Collection

PAGE 11
Alphonse Legros
*Mountain Landscape with
two Figures at the Right*, 1905
Watercolor over pen and brown ink;
10¼ × 18½ in. (25.9 × 46.9 cm)
National Academy of Art; Gift of
George Matthew Adams in memory
of his mother, Lydia Havens Adams

PAGE 12
Isabel Quintanilla Martinez
The Red Door, 1978
Oil on panel; 64⅝ × 42½ in.
(164 × 108 cm)
Private Collection, Germany
© Isabel Quintanilla, VEGAP, Madrid,
2024

PAGE 15
Eadweard Muybridge
*Plate number 156. Jumping, running
straight high jump* (detail), 1887
Collotype; 7¼ ×16⅞ in. (18.2 × 42.9 cm)
National Gallery of Art, Corcoran
Collection

PAGES 16-17
Konstantinos Kyrtis
Juno, 2022
Oil on linen; 40½ × 36 in. (103 × 92 cm)
Private Collection

PAGE 18
Ben Bauer
On Winter Walks, Scandinavian, MN,
2022
Oil and cold wax on linen; 24 × 26 in.
(61 × 66 cm)
Private Collection

PAGE 21
John Ruskin
Champagnole, 1846
Watercolor, graphite, and white
gouache on wove paper; 5 × 7 in.
(12.7 × 17.8 cm)
Yale Center for British Art; Given in
honor of Patrick Noon, Curator of
Prints, Drawings & Rare Books, from
the collection of Iola S. Haverstick

PAGE 24
Robert Gherardi
Muted in Song
Acrylic on board; 10 × 8 in.
(25.4 × 20.3 cm)
17th International Art Renewal
Center Salon

PAGE 26
John Constable
Cloud Study: Stormy Sunset, 1821-22
Oil on paper on canvas; 8 × 10¾ in.
(20.3 × 27.3 cm)
National Gallery of Art; Gift of
Louise Mellon in honor of
Mr. and Mrs. Paul Mellon

PAGES 28-29
José de Ribera
Studies of Eyes, c. 1622
Etching with plate-tone on paper;
5⅝ × 8½ in (14.3 × 21.6 cm)
British Museum

PAGE 30
Edward Burne-Jones
*Theseus and the Minotaur in the
Labyrinth, design for a painted tile*, 1861
Pencil, brown wash, pen, and ink
on paper; 10 × 10¼ in. (25.5 × 26.1 cm)
Birmingham City Museum and
Art Gallery

PAGES 34-35
Caspar David Friedrich
Riesengebirge, c. 1830-35
Oil on canvas; 28⅜ × 40¼ in. (72 × 102 cm)
Nationalgalerie, Staatlichen Museen
zu Berlin
Image courtesy of Art Renewal Center

PAGE 36
Paul Dubois
Joan d'Arc, 1873
Black stone and charcoal on vellum;
sheet 13½ x 10⅜ in. (34.3 × 26.5 cm)
Musée des Beaux-Arts de Reims

PAGE 40
Juliette Aristides
Mastercopy of geometric proportions of the Farnese Hercules (from the de Ganay Manuscript) after Peter Paul Rubens, 2023
Pen in brown ink on toned paper; 6 x 8 in.
Artist's Collection

PAGE 42
Charles Weed
Shell on Grey Green, 2023
Oil on panel; 16½ × 19¾ in. (42 × 50 cm)
Image courtesy of Ann Long Fine Art

PAGE 44
Stanislaw Wyspiański
Sketches of an eye, 1887/1888
Pencil on paper, sketchbook page 87 (verso); 6½ × 4 in. (16.4 × 10.2 cm)
National Museum in Krakow, Stanisław Wyspiański Collection

PAGE 46
Richard Greathouse
La Giovane Dottoressa, 2018
Oil on linen; 21¾ × 19¾ in. (55.24 × 50.16 cm)
Private Collection

PAGE 48
Andrea del Verrocchio
Measured Drawing of a Horse Facing Left (recto)
Pen and dark brown ink, over traces of black chalk, ca. 1480–88
9 13/16 x 11 11/16 in. (24.9 x 29.7 cm)
Frederick C. Hewitt Fund, 1917
Metropolitan Museum of Art

PAGE 51
Marcos Rey
Mujer de piedra (detail in process), 2017
Charcoal, ink, wash, and oil on canvas; 33½ × 30⅜ in. (85 × 77 cm)
Private Collection

PAGE 52 (LEFT)
Juliette Aristides
Mastercopy of geometric proportions of the Farnese Hercules (from the de Ganay Manuscript) after Peter Paul Rubens, no date
Pen in brown ink on laid paper; no dimensions
Rubenshuis, Antwerp
Artist's Collection

PAGE 52 (RIGHT)
Marble bust of a man, mid-1st century CE
Marble; h. 14⅜ in. (36.5 cm)
Metropolitan Museum of Art; Rogers Fund, 1912

PAGE 53 (LEFT)
Balthasar Denner
Portrait of an Old Woman, 1720–45
Oil on copper; 14¾ × 12⅜ in. (37.5 × 31.5 cm)
Hermitage Museum

PAGE 53 (RIGHT)
Johannes Vermeer
Study of a Young Woman, c. 1665–67
Oil on canvas; 17½ × 15¾ in. (44.5 × 40 cm)
Metropolitan Museum of Art; Gift of Mr. and Mrs. Charles Wrightsman, in memory of Theodore Rousseau Jr., 1979

PAGE 54
Scott Conary
Heavy Glow, 2022
Oil on panel; 13 × 13 in. (33 × 33 cm)
Private Collection

PAGE 56
Jeffery Larson
Sea Shell, 2020
Oil on linen; 16 × 16 in. (40.6 × 40.6 cm)
Private Collection

PAGE 58
Deborah Paris
Dusk, Edge of the Woods, 2013
Oil on linen; 18 × 24 in. (45.7 × 61 cm)
Collection of Dave and Mallory Agerton, Houston, Texas

PAGE 59:
Gary Faigin
Three Objects on a Red Tablecloth, 2000s
Oil on canvas board; 18 × 24 in. (45.7 × 61 cm)
Private Collection

PAGE 61
Carlo Russo
Estella Rijnveld, 2021
Oil on panel; 10 × 8 in. (25.4 × 20.3 cm)
Private Collection

PAGES 62 (DETAILS) AND PAGE 63
Pieter Bruegel the Elder
The Fall of Icarus, 1560
Oil on panel; 29 × 44 in. (73.7 × 111.8 cm)
Royal Museums of Fine Arts of Belgium, Museum of Fine Arts

PAGE 64
John Singer Sargent
Rehearsal of the Pasdeloup Orchestra at the Cirque d'Hiver, c. 1879–80
Oil on canvas; 22½ × 18⅛ in. (57.2 × 46 cm)
Museum of Fine Arts, Boston; The Hayden Collection–Charles Henry Hayden Fund
Photograph © 2025 Museum of Fine Arts, Boston.

PAGES 66–67
Marcos Rey
Mar, 2017
Charcoal, ink, and wash; 29½ × 21¾ in. (75 × 55 cm)
Private Collection

PAGE 68
John Ruskin
The South Side of St Mark's from the Loggia of the Ducal Palace, Venice (detail), c. 1851
Watercolor over pencil heightened with white, on 3 pieces of paper; 38 × 18 in. (96 × 46 cm)
Private Collection

PAGE 71 (LEFT)
Francesco di Giorgio Martini
Figure with proportions, 1470
From *Trattato di architettura di Francesco di Giorgio Martini*

PAGE 71 (RIGHT)
Francesco di Giorgio Martini
Illustration of an Architrave, no date
From *Trattato di architettura di Francesco di Giorgio Martini*

PAGE 72 (LEFT)
Egg yolk photographed by Greg Nyssen

PAGE 72 (MIDDLE)
Hoag's Object ring galaxy
Taken by the Hubble Space Telescope, July 2001
Image Credit: NASA, R. Lucas (STScI/AURA)

PAGE 72 (RIGHT)
Interior of the rose window at Strasbourg Cathedral

PAGE 75
Kenny Harris
Hall of Mirrors, Havana, 2016
Oil on canvas
20 × 16 in. (50.8 × 40.6 cm)
Private Collection

PAGE 76
Diagram on front façade of Santa Maria Novella in Florence, Italy

PAGE 77
Front façade of Santa Croce in Florence, Italy

PAGE 78
Barry Bub photograph
www.BarryBubPhotography.com

PAGE 80
Patrick Okrasinski
San Niccolo, 2023
Oil on linen; 12 × 9 in. (30.6 × 22.9 cm)
Private Collection

PAGE 83
Rembrandt van Rijn
Self-portrait, 1655
Oil on linen; 19¾ × 16¾ in. (50 × 42.5 cm)
National Gallery of Scotland, Bridgewater Collection loan

PAGE 85
Photograph of Buddha sculpture at the Frye Art Museum by Juliette Aristides

PAGES 86-87
Edmund George Warren
Leith Hill from Broadmoor, Surrey, 1860
Watercolor with pen and ink and gum arabic; 14 × 20 in. (35.5 × 50.7 cm)
Metropolitan Museum of Art; Purchase, Friends of Drawings and Prints Gifts, 2019

PAGE 88
Claude Monet
Morning on the Seine, near Giverny (detail), 1897
Oil on canvas; 32 × 36½ in. (81.3 × 92.7 cm)
Museum of Fine Arts Boston;
Gift of Mrs. Walter Scott Fitz
Photograph ©2025 Museum of Fine Arts, Boston.

PAGE 92
Henry Ossawa Tanner
The Disciples See Christ Walking on the Water, 1907
Oil on canvas; 51½ × 42 in. (130.8 × 106.7 cm)
Des Moines Art Center

PAGE 94
Kenny Harris
Chair with Linen Curtains, 2019
Oil on panel; 10 × 8 in. (25.4 × 20.3 cm)
Private Collection

PAGE 96
Juliette Aristides
The Forest, 2023
Mixed drawing media on toned paper; 27 × 19 in. (68.6 × 48.3 cm)
Private Collection

PAGE 98:
Caspar David Friedrich
Walk at Dusk (Man Contemplating a Megalith), c. 1830-35
Oil on canvas; 13¼ × 17 in. (33.7 × 43.2 cm)
John Paul Getty Museum

PAGE 100
Letter from Wilson MacDonald to Levin Coburn Handy, dated April 8, 1895
Ink on paper; 9½ × $5\frac{15}{16}$ in. (24.1 × 15.1 cm)
National Portrait Gallery, Smithsonian Institution; gift of Claire Kaland

PAGES 101-103
Script examples by Marie Hornback, teacher and calligrapher
www.crowncalligraphy.com;
IG: @crown.calligraphy

PAGE 104
Patrick Byrnes
Freddy en Violet, 2021
Colored pencil on paper; 11½ × 8 in. (29.2 × 20.3 cm)
Collection of the artist

PAGE 107
Konstantinos Kyrtis
Juno, 2022
Oil on linen; 40½ × 36 in. (103 × 92 cm)
Private Collection

PAGE 109
Jusepe de Ribera
Studies of Two Ears and of a Bat, no date
Red chalk and brush and red wash on beige paper; 6¼ × 11 in. (15.9 × 27.9 cm)
Metropolitan Museum of Art;
Rogers Fund, 1972

PAGE 110
Mario Robinson
Kenyatta, 2000
Pastel on paper; 16 × 16 in. (40.6 × 40.6 cm)
Private Collection

PAGE 112
Amaya Gurpide
The last strands of winter, 2015
Mixed media on hand-toned paper mounted on dibond; 8 × 6 in. (20.3 × 15.2 cm)
Private Collection

PAGES 116-117
John Frederick Kensett
Sunset on the Sea, 1872
Oil on canvas; 28 × 41⅛ in. (71.1 × 104.5 cm)
Metropolitan Museum of Art;
Gift of Thomas Kensett, 1874

PAGE 118
Marek Yanai
Entrance in the German Colony, Jerusalem, 2004
Oil on canvas; 55 × 39⅜ in. (140 × 100 cm)
Private Collection

PAGE 120
Ellen Eagle
Mei-Chiao, 2002
Pastel on pumice board; 6½ × 6¾ in. (16.5 × 15.9 cm)
Private Collection

PAGE 122
Paul Seaton
Antique Roses, Silver and Silk, 2020
Oil on linen; 18 x 14 in. (45.7 × 35.6 cm)
Image Courtesy of Collins Galleries

PAGE 126
Rachel Li
The Silk Wrap, 2021
Oil on panel; 18 × 24 in. (45.7 × 61 cm)
Private Collection

CLOSING ENDPAPER
Ryan Brown
Moonlit Lake, 2020
Oil on linen; 18 × 24 in. (45.7 × 61 cm)
Private Collection

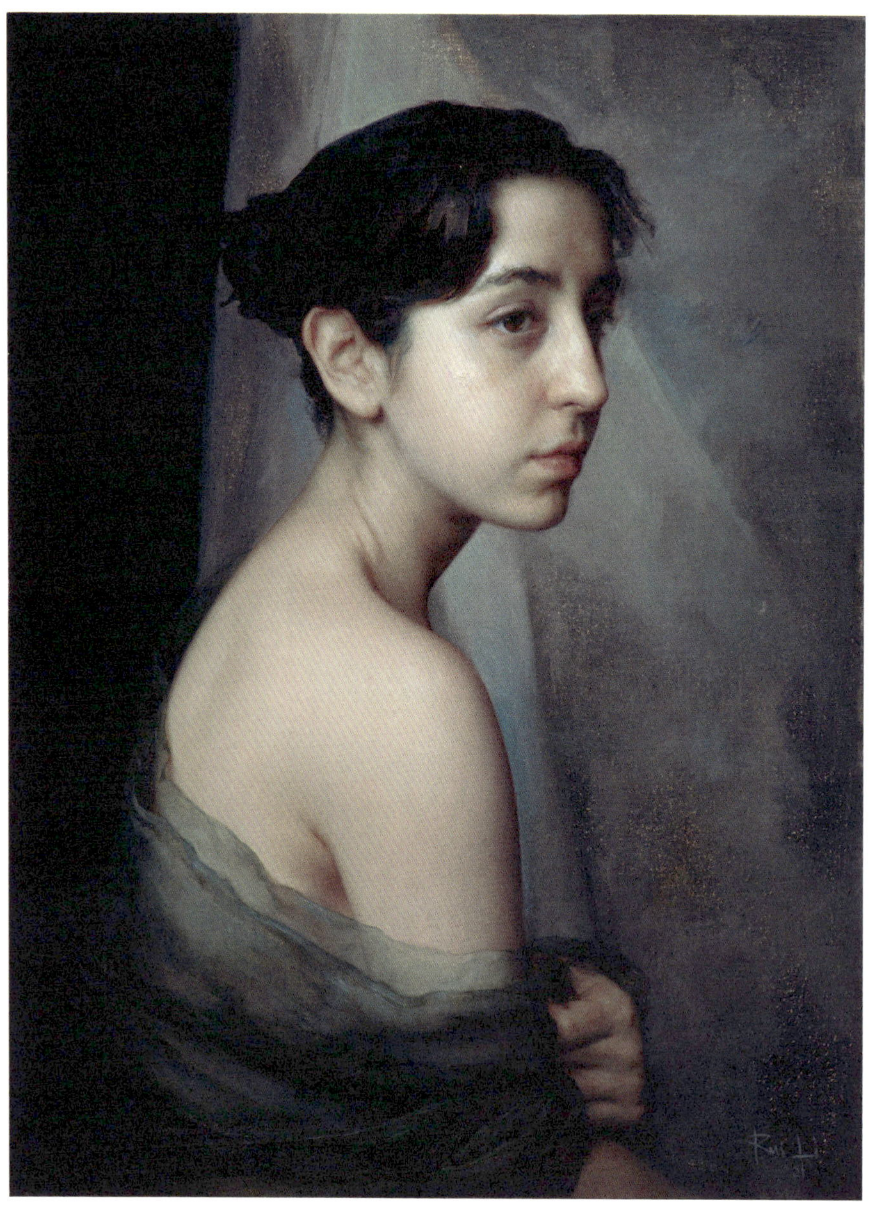

ENLARGE YOUR INNER LIFE

Slow down
Go inward
Keep a sketchbook
Notice what calls your attention
Find hidden things that give you pleasure
Have long conversations
Choose your mentors
Read often
Read deeply
Turn toward inspiration
Collect quotes
Learn to draw
Write bad poetry
See art in person
Let your mind wander
Let your feet wander
Look for beauty in the least likely places

—JULIETTE ARISTIDES

EDITOR: Carla Sakamoto
DESIGNER: Jessica Fleischmann / Still Room
PRODUCTION DIRECTOR: Michael Vagnetti
COVER DESIGN BY Jessica Fleischmann / Still Room

Library of Congress Control Number: 2024950479

ISBN: 978-1-58093-657-6

Printed in China

Monacelli
A Phaidon Company
111 Broadway
New York, NY 10006

www.phaidon.com/monacelli

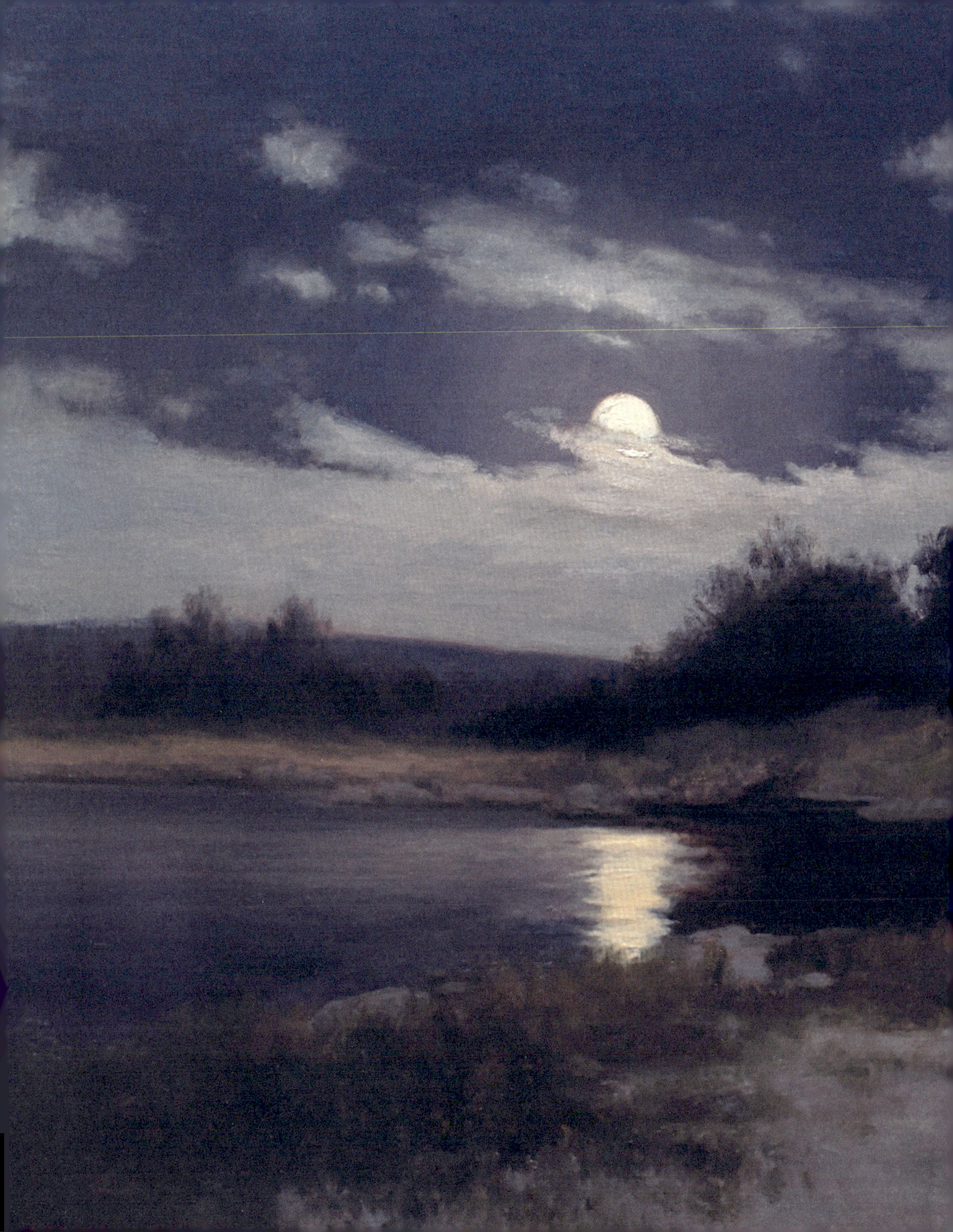